BIBLIOTHERAPY
WITH STEPCHILDREN

BIBLIOTHERAPY WITH STEPCHILDREN

By

MARILYN COLEMAN, ED.D.

Child and Family Development
University of Missouri - Columbia

LAWRENCE H. GANONG, PH.D.

Child and Family Development and
School of Nursing
University of Missouri - Columbia

CHARLES C THOMAS • PUBLISHER
Springfield • Illinois • U.S.A.

Published and Distributed Throughout the World by

CHARLES C THOMAS • PUBLISHER

2600 South First Street

Springfield, Illinois 62794-9265

© *1988 by* CHARLES C THOMAS • PUBLISHER

ISBN 0-398-05485-1

Library of Congress Catalog Card Number: 88-6523

With **THOMAS BOOKS** *careful attention is given to all details of manufacturing and
design. It is the Publisher's desire to present books that are satisfactory as to their physical
qualities and artistic possibilities and appropriate for their particular use.* THOMAS
BOOKS *will be true to those laws of quality that assure a good name and good will.*

Printed in the United States of America

Q-R-3

Library of Congress Cataloging in Publication Data

Coleman, Marilyn.
    Bibliotherapy with stepchildren / by Marilyn Coleman,
Lawrence H. Ganong.
       p.   cm.
    Bibliography: p.
    Includes index.
    ISBN 0-398-5485-1
    1. Bibliotherapy for children. 2. Bibliotherapy.
3. Stepchildren--Mental health. 4. Stepchildren--Book reviews.
I. Ganong, Lawrence H. II. Title.
RJ505.B5C65 1988
618.92′89166--dc19
                                  88-6523
                                  CIP

PREFACE

THIS BOOK had an innocent beginning as a class project by one of our students in a course on Remarriage and Stepparenting that we co-teach at the University of Missouri. The student, Susan Marshall Roberts, was a reading specialist who was working on a doctorate in education. She was seeking a project that would connect her love of reading and her professional area of expertise with the topic of stepfamilies. Her idea: To read and abstract novels for adolescents that had a "step" theme. Thinking this a good idea, and believing it to be a manageable project that Susan could easily complete during the semester (probably there weren't more than a dozen or so books we thought), we encouraged her to begin.

The handful of books we expected to find grew to be dozens and dozens. Susan took a grade of "incomplete" so that she could finish the project, Marilyn soon became interested in reading some of this fiction, and before long Larry was involved as well. Eventually, fiction for preadolescents and self-help books for children and adolescents were added.

Over the last few years we have become the "stepfamily reviewers," having reviewed a number of bodies of literature focusing on remarriage and stepfamilies, including self-help books for adults (Coleman, Ganong, & Gingrich, 1985; Coleman, Ganong, & Gingrich, 1986), empirical research (Ganong & Coleman, 1984), clinical work (Ganong & Coleman, 1986), and college textbooks (Nolan, Coleman, & Ganong, 1984). It was a logical step for us to begin to systematically analyze and review the fiction and self-help literature for stepchildren.

When we were about two-thirds through the project we presented some of our impressions to a group of interested persons at a Stepfamily Conference at the University of Iowa. After our talk, we were mobbed by counselors, teachers, clergy, stepparents, and others who wanted to know how they could get the information from us. We weren't done, we protested, and, besides, we were not at all sure what we would do with this. At the conference we were presenting some loosely-developed ideas about how these books might be used. The reactions of the participants struck a chord; obviously, these books could be used by a variety of people to help stepchildren and others.

We are clinicians and teachers and stepfamily members. It did not take long for us to recognize the ways literature can be used by stepfamily members and by people who work with them. The result is this book.

The goals of this book are: (1) to present ways self-help literature and fiction can be used by parents, teachers, counselors, and others, and (2) to present the content of self-help and fictional literature available for stepchildren. We have extensively examined all the self-help literature and most of the fiction for children and adolescents.

The audiences we are writing for are as broad as the literature we read. One group are professionals engaged in counseling stepchildren. This group includes counselors, clergy, social workers, psychiatrists, psychologists, family therapists, and others. The second group are professionals engaged in educational or preventive work, such as teachers, family life educators, and librarians. The third group consists of adults in stepfamilies.

How to Use This Book

We have planned this book to be useable. It should be a convenient reference book that readers can consult when seeking particular kinds of information, such as which self-help books discuss loyalty conflicts or what novels portray stepsibling relationships. It may also be read in its entirety, however, by those with a more academic bent or by those who want to really know all about current literature for and about stepchildren.

Chapter 1 is a brief review of common issues and concerns facing stepchildren and their families. This chapter should be helpful to professionals who are not members of stepfamilies themselves and who have not worked extensively with stepfamilies. This may even be an informative chapter for stepfamily adults; often what may seem to be obvious characteristics of stepfamilies are not so obvious to members of such family systems. This "scholarly" chapter has been written so that it may be read and appreciated by nonprofessionals as well as professionals.

Chapter 2 contains a discussion of bibliotherapy in general, as well as some suggestions regarding the specific use of fiction and self-help books with stepparents and stepchildren. This chapter also presents some ideas on choosing stepfamily literature for children and adolescents. Some of these ideas were gleaned from other authors who have used biblioeducation methods with other groups. Most of the criteria discussed in this chapter, however, is based on our own research and teaching with stepfamily members and the work of several of our colleagues who work with stepfamilies.

Chapters 3 and 4 describe the fiction and self-help literature review projects. Sampling techniques, methods and criteria for reviewing, and methods of analyzing are explained. This information is important, since it is necessary for readers to estimate how valid and reliable the reviews are. In these chapters we also summarize our general impressions and conclusions about the stepfamily self-help and fiction literature for children and adolescents. In addition, annotations of each work are provided.

Following Chapter 4 is a section called the Classification Guide. The Classification Guide provides a listing of the authors and titles of the 265 books reviewed. The date of publication as well as the publisher is included as well. The age and sex of the main character/s is provided in this section along with a rating of the literary quality of each book. The final item included in this section is information regarding the centrality to the book of stepfamily issues and themes.

The final section is entitled Book Summaries and Coding. This section provides a very brief summary of each book, notations about the type of stepfamily (stepmother, stepfather, or both, etc.), common stepfamily themes present in each book, the suggested age range of readers and whether or not we recommend the book.

This project has been extremely time consuming, but it has been a labor of love. Stepfamilies and stepfamily members have been negatively stereotyped for a long time through media (Visher & Visher, 1982). With the high rate of remarriage and subsequent formation of many stepfamilies, now seemed the appropriate time to thoroughly explore the quantity and quality of available media. We discovered that self-help books are finally moving beyond first person accounts, and the literature for children has moved past Snow White and Cinderella. Books are available that can be very helpful to the ever-expanding group needing to understand the underlying dynamics of stepfamily living.

The self-help books present a wealth of useful information on how to maximize step living and the fictional work presents some unforgettable stepfamily characters. As with most bodies of work, however, the gems are only a fraction of the whole. In this book we have highlighted the gems — those books destined to be classics in a positive mode just as Cinderella has been a classic of negative stepfamily stereotyping for centuries.

References

Coleman, M., Ganong, L., & Gingrich, R. (1985). Stepfamily strengths: A review of the popular literature. *Family Relations, 34,* 583-589.

Coleman, M., Ganong, L., & Gingrich, R. (1986). Strengths of stepfamilies identified in professional literature. In S. Van Zandt (Ed.), *Building family strengths (Vol. 7)* (pp. 429-451). Lincoln, NB. University of Nebraska press.

Ganong, L., & Coleman, M. (1984). Effects of remarriage on children: A review of the empirical literature. *Family Relations, 33,* 389-406.

Ganong, L., & Coleman, M. (1986). A comparison of clinical and empirical literature on children in stepfamilies. *Journal of Marriage and the Family, 48,* 309-318.

Nolan, J., Coleman, M., & Ganong, L. (1984). The presentation of stepfamilies in marriage and family textbooks. *Family Relations, 33,* 559-566.

Visher, J., & Visher, E. (1982). Stepfamilies and stepparenting. In N. Walsh (Ed.), *Normal family processes* (pp. 331-353). New York: Guilford.

CONTENTS

BIBLIOTHERAPY
WITH STEPCHILDREN

CHAPTER 1

STEP ISSUES AND CONCERNS

WHAT DO George Washington, actor Tom Selleck, novelist John Irving, and Drs. Seuss and Spock have in common? What similarity links First Lady Nancy Reagan, Whistler's Mother, and Yoko Ono? What do Abraham Lincoln, Gerald Ford, Erik Erikson, baseball pitcher Dan Quisenberry, columnist Russell Baker, and actors Burt Reynolds and Christopher Reeve share? What do all the aforementioned people have in common? Answer: All belonged to a stepfamily at some point in their lives, either as a stepparent, such as George Washington and Nancy Reagan, or as a stepchild, such as Abraham Lincoln and Russell Baker. Some, like First Lady Nancy Reagan, grew up in a stepfamily and then found themselves as an adult in the stepparent role. These famous Americans of the past and present share a "step" status with a growing number of individuals.

The relatively high rates of divorce and remarriage have resulted in a large, and growing, number of stepfamilies in the United States. At the present time, approximately 50% of first marriages end in divorce (Glick, 1984). Of these divorced individuals, nearly 80% remarry within 3 to 5 years (Glick, 1984). Many of these remarrying adults have children, thus creating stepfamilies.

A stepfamily, often known as a blended, reconstituted, or remarried family, is one in which at least one of the adults has a child (or children) from a previous relationship. A stepparent is an adult who marries a person who has had a child (or children) from a previous relationship. A stepchild is a child whose parent (or parents) are married to someone who is not the child's biological parent. Notice that these definitions do not limit stepfamily status to those who reside in the same household. A stepparent and stepchild may not live together all of the time or even part of the time to have a relationship together and to share stepfamily membership. In fact, with joint legal and physical custody of children becoming more prevalent, children's membership in two households is an increasingly common reality. Thus, a remarried household may be "linked" to another remarried household or to a single-parent household by children (Jacobson, 1984) and these "binuclear" households may contain several combinations of full- and part-time step relationships (Ahrons & Perlmutter, 1982). If one considers custody of children and stepparent combinations (i.e. stepmother, stepfather, both), a possibility of 32 types of stepfamily configurations exist (Wald, 1981).

How many "steps" are there? Census Bureau data are not available and estimates vary widely, but even the most conservative estimates indicate that there are many. Cherlin and McCarthy (1985) calculated that there are nearly 2½ million households that are post-divorce stepfamilies with residential children. To this number must be added an unknown percentage of post-bereavement remarrieds and those single-parent households that are linked to stepfamily households. At any one time, about 10% of American children live with a stepfather and mother (Bumpass, 1984; Glick, 1984) and about 2% with a stepmother and father (Bachrach, 1983). If current divorce and remarriage rates continue, as many as 25% to 30% of the children will be part of a stepfamily before they are 19 years old (Glick, 1984).

Stepfamily Characteristics

Stepfamilies are quite different from first-marriage, or nuclear families. Even when stepfamilies appear structurally to be the same as a nuclear family (e.g., the household contains a mom, a dad, and children) they are different in several important ways:

1. Stepfamilies are more complex.
2. All members have different family histories.
3. Parent-child bonds are older than spouse bonds.
4. Stepfamilies are less supported by the society as a whole.

Complexity. As a group, stepfamilies are complex units with characteristics that deserve special consideration. To begin with, stepfamilies often have more adults and children than nuclear families. Remarriages following divorce may result in four adults in parental positions: a mother, a stepfather, a father, and a stepmother. Between the two households there may be several sets of "his" and "hers" children, as well as the possibility of an "ours" child if the remarried couples reproduce. The greater number of people adds complexity to stepfamilies. More people means more relationships and more relationships put a stress on communication between members.

Stepfamilies also are complex because of the unique roles. The roles and responsibilities of stepmothers and stepfathers are poorly defined in our culture (Cherlin, 1978). Much has been written about the struggle stepparents and their spouses have in deciding how much a stepparents' role functioning will mimic that of a parent in a nuclear family (Visher & Visher, 1979). Various alternatives, such as "parent," "other parent," and "nonparent" have been discussed but remarried adults have few guidelines to follow in developing a stepparent role (Cherlin, 1978). Other roles and role definition problems add to the complexity of stepfamilies as well. Few guidelines exist to aid stepsons, stepdaughters, stepsiblings, stepgrandparents, and halfsiblings. How are former spouses to relate to each other? The roles of noncustodial parent and stepparent and nonresidential stepsibling are even less well-defined. Developing comfortable and workable roles and relationships is difficult; this task adds to stepfamily complexity.

Another complicating factor is that stepchildren may hold membership in two households. This may range from almost full-time residence in one household with only occasional visits to the other household to half-time residence in both. Most stepchildren probably fall in between these two extremes, residing mostly with one parent but spending some time periodically with the other parent. The increase in prevalence of joint legal and physical custody in recent years may result in more stepchildren being part-time members of two households. Pragmatically, when children have membership in two households it means that stepfamily households find themselves gaining and losing children from time to time. A remarried couple can find themselves with an empty nest one weekend, have two children to raise during the week, and the next weekend have a house full of four children. This accordion effect contains logistical and emotional complications for adults and children. Children who go back and forth may find themselves adjusting to different sets of rules and expectations.

The greater complexity of stepfamilies, it should be noted, does not imply that these are inherently problematic and distressful. Although the tendency has been for our culture to assume that deviations from the nuclear family are bad, the difference in complexity may be an asset to some families and individuals and a deficit to others.

Different Histories. Another unique characteristic of stepfamilies is that family members have different family histories from each other. Adults in nuclear families enter marriage with their own family-of-origin histories, but they go on to develop a mutual family culture with it's own history, rituals, and traditions. Children raised in nuclear families share that history as part of a common family culture. In stepfamilies, a parent and child(ren) have mutual experiences and shared recollections of a family life that does not include the stepparent (and any children he or she may have). This is important not only because some stepfamily members are excluded from "remember when . . . " anecdotes, but because different histories can result in patterns of living or lifestyles that seem odd to stepfamily members who have not been part of the evolution of those patterns. This joining of culture may cause confusion in the period of transition following remarriage and if not resolved, may result in a chronic sense that things don't feel right and "natural" in the stepfamily (Goldner, 1982). Different ways of "being a family," can lead to misunderstandings and mistaken assumptions. This process of merging two lifestyles puts a premium on communicating expectations clearly and being flexible in adapting.

Parent-Child Predates Couple. Another major characteristic that distinguishes stepfamilies from nuclear families, is that the parent-child bond is formed prior to the marital bond. This may mean, in addition to the shared history differences mentioned above, that the primary emotional tie for newly remarried parents is with their child(ren) rather than with their new spouse. Unlike first-time marriages, couples in stepfamilies must develop a marital unit at the same time they are maintaining parent-child relationships and beginning stepparent-child ties. At least in the early periods of stepfamily life, it is not unreasonable to assume that primary loyalty for parents will be to their child rather than to their spouse. Remarriages by people with children do not have the luxury of months and years alone to adjust to each other like people do in first marriages.

Stepfamilies Are Fragile

Stepfamilies are obviously different from nuclear families. What effect do these differences have? We hope we made the point clearly earlier in this chapter that differences do not automatically mean that stepfamilies are inherently fraught with problems. Many stepfamilies function well, and are nurturing environments for both children and adults.

Stepfamilies, however, present challenges that seem to overwhelm many. Stepfamilies are more fragile systems than nuclear families. The divorce rate is higher in stepfamilies (Glick, 1984) probably because they seem to have additional opportunities for problems and distress (Visher & Visher, 1979).

Remarriage Effects on Children

What is the effect of parental remarriage on children? In the past, it was popularly assumed that parental remarriage had a detrimental effect on children. One indication of this perspective is that "step-child" has become a metaphor for something abused, neglected, or unloved: "stepparent" (especially "stepmother") has become a negative term laden with stereotypes (e.g., stepmothers are wicked and mean). Portrayals of wicked stepmothers and abusive stepfathers in fairy tales are perhaps other indications of the popular assumption that stepchildren are likely to exhibit mental, emotional, and interpersonal problems.

Popular assumptions and stereotypes aside, the important question remains: What is the effect of parental remarriage on children? Researchers and clinicians tend to disagree on the answer (Ganong & Coleman, 1986). Researchers, in general, have reported little evidence that children in stepfamilies differ significantly from children from other family structures in cognitive development, self-image, and social relationships. Research results are more mixed regarding mental health and family relationships, but the preponderance of studies find few differences between stepchildren and other children in these areas as well (Ganong & Coleman, 1984). Clinical writers, on the other hand, have identified several negative, and a few positive, effects of parental remarriage on children (Ganong & Coleman, 1986). These differences in conclusions drawn by researchers and clinicians are due to differences in methods of seeking answers and in sampling differences. Without deciding which group has more validity (actually both have much to offer in helping one gain an understanding of stepfamilies and stepchildren), we will focus on problems and strengths identified by clinicians in the rest of this chapter. Clinicians have based their conclusions on families who have sought help for individual or family problems; the issues identified are thus likely to be ones that would be useful to the stepfamily members and practitioners who would use this book.

Issues Facing Stepchildren and Their Families

Problems and adjustments encountered by stepchildren will be presented in five conceptual clusters: Family Dynamics, Transitional Adjustments, Incomplete Institution, Emotional Responses, and Stepfamily Expectations.

Family Dynamics. This is an area of great importance for stepchildren and their families. Family dynamics can be viewed as covering three groups: (a) the stepfamily household, (b) the household of the "other" parent, and (c) extended family kin.

Stepfamily Household Dynamics. Discipline is a frequent problem in stepfamilies, particularly in the early periods following remarriage when family members are still unsure of the household rules (Messenger, 1984). Discipline problems can include value differences between parent and stepparent, children reacting negatively to the stepparent's efforts to discipline them, perceived inequities in punishments, and discrepant expectations regarding proper behavior for children. Conflicts over discipline can be among the most difficult to resolve. Several other problems are related to conflicts over discipline. Children rejecting the stepparent is one such outcome (Jacobson, 1979), stepparents rejecting a meaningful relationship with the stepchild is another (Podolsky, 1955), and, perhaps most seriously, the expulsion of stepchildren from the stepfamily household is another (Crohn, et al., 1982).

Discipline conflicts, and other parenting concerns, have an impact on the marital relationship between the parent and stepparent (Sager, et al., 1983). Marital problems can, in turn, affect stepchildren; children can become triangled into marital disputes (Friedman, 1981 and Whiteside, 1982); or they may become scapegoats for unresolved conflict in the remarriage (Whiteside, 1981).

We noted earlier in this chapter that stepfamilies are sometimes called blended or reconstituted families. An implicit expectation of both those labels is that the stepfamily following the remarriage will be as close as a first-marriage family and the basic dynamics will be similar to nuclear families. Remarried adults are frequently guilty of expecting more cohesion and closeness than children are comfortable with (McGoldrick & Carter, 1980). This push for cohesion stresses children (Kompara, 1980), and can result in pseudomutuality, an unwillingness to honestly express disagreements (McGoldrick & Carter, 1980), or rebellion and withdrawal by children (Sager, et al., 1983). As an unintended result of this adult push for cohesion, stepfamilies end up with less cohesion because children pull away (McGoldrick & Carter, 1980; Visher & Visher, 1979).

Stepsibling relations can also be a source of problems (Gardner, 1984). Stepsibs may not get along for a variety of reasons, including personality clashes, rivalry for parent's attention, competition for scarce household resources, jealousy, changes in birth order positions, and resistance to sexual attraction. The addition of halfsiblings may also stimulate rivalry, jealousy and the feeling of being an outsider (Maddox, 1975).

Names can be a subtle source of tension in stepfamilies. Children sometimes are confused about what to call a stepparent (Wald, 1981). Parents may unthinkingly push children to use terms like "mom" and "dad" when addressing stepparents without considering the children's feelings about it. We have talked to stepchildren in their early twenties who were still bitter about being forced to call a stepparent mom or dad when they were younger. If the use of such terms are important to adults, children learn to use the labels as a way to manipulate stepparents. For example, one stepson told us that when he wanted something from his stepmother he always called her "mom" because he knew it pleased her and she was more likely to give him what he wanted. Having different last names can also create some problems, such as embarrassment in front of peers and making a child with a different last name from other family members feel like an outsider.

Space issues affect family dynamics as stepfamilies try to combine two units together (Stanton, 1986). Nonresidential stepchildren need to feel like they own some space in the household and residential children need to feel like they are not being invaded and pushed aside by visiting stepsibs (Stanton, 1986).

Binuclear Family Dynamics. Many families following divorce are becoming binuclear families, families that consist of divorced former spouses who reside in separate households and their children who share residence part-time in both houses (Ahrons & Perlmutter, 1982). When a parent remarries, this binuclear living pattern can create difficulties for stepfamily members. Coparental conflicts may begin or may increase following the remarriage of a former spouse (Whiteside, 1983). Custody issues that had been apparently resolved may flair again (Crohn, et al., 1982). Children may experience loyalty conflicts between parent and stepparent and biological parent-child ties may become strained (Sager, et al., 1983; Visher & Visher, 1979). Children may also feel tension trying to bridge membership in two households (Greif, 1982); this tension can be heightened when parents and children disagree over family boundaries (who is in or not in the family) or when family boundaries are too vague for most member's comfort (Crohn, et al., 1982).

Transitional Adjustment. Clinicians have written most extensively about stepchildren's adjustments to parental remarriage (Ganong & Coleman, 1986). Getting used to the inevitable changes that occur following remarriage is a major task. Some children have a harder time adapting to changes in their routines than others; obviously, children who are more flexible and adaptable will make a smoother transition to stepfamily living. Several variables seem to be related to the necessity for stepchildren to make major adjustments: lifestyle differences between the child and new stepparent (Sager, et al., 1983), birth order changes for the child (McGoldrick & Carter, 1980), a short time between parental death or divorce and remarriage (Visher & Visher, 1979), the child not being told of the remarriage (Wald, 1981), and the child being an adolescent when the parent remarries (McGoldrick & Carter, 1980). It is probably unavoidable that members of the new unit will lack shared family rituals (Goldner, 1982; Visher & Visher, 1982) and rules (Whiteside, 1983) in the early period following remarriage. Conflict during the merging period happens as new stepfamily members become used to each other's different styles (McGoldrick & Carter, 1980; Wald, 1981). For example, little things like where food should be stored in the refrigerator and how children should ask to be excused from the table can be fuel for blazing arguments.

Sometimes adjustment to parental remarriage is made more difficult because of a mistaken belief on the part of stepparents and parents that stepchildren and stepparents will instantly love each other. Called "the myth of instant love" (Visher & Visher, 1982), this belief leads to disappointment, frustration, and sometimes anger when the expectation of immediate love is not met.

Incomplete Institution. Some problems stepchildren experience are due to the lack of societal institutionalization of remarried families (Cherlin, 1978). In other words, stepfamilies do not have the advantage of "automatically" knowing how to fulfill their roles since stepfamilies lack societal norms to guide them. This can result in role confusion (Fast & Cain, 1967), family identity confusion (Ahrons & Perlmutter, 1982), and, because there is no model for stepparent-child relations, confusion about how much affection to show (Mowatt, 1972) and how to show affection between stepmembers (Fast & Cain, 1967) can be chronic problems. Even the absence of legal ties between stepchildren and stepparents (Fishman & Hamel, 1981), the dearth of kinship terms for step-relationships (Jones, 1978), and the lack of societal rituals to support stepfamilies (Goldner, 1982; Jacobson, 1979) can result in headaches for stepchildren and their families.

Emotional Responses. Clinical writers tend to agree that certain emotional reactions and feelings are generally common among stepchildren (Ganong & Coleman, 1986). A sense of loss is perhaps the most frequently mentioned response; stepchildren mourn for the loss of contact with a deceased or noncustodial parent, for a lost family life, perhaps for a lost feeling of stability, for a house or friends they may have had to leave following parental remarriage (Sager, et al., 1983; Visher & Visher, 1979). Children may mourn for lost closeness with their newly remarried parent and they may feel saddened at the reduced possibility that their fantasies of parental reunification will become reality (Visher & Visher, 1982). Anger at parents and stepparents is said to be common (Isaacs, 1982), as are feelings of ambivalence towards the new stepfamily (Walker & Messinger, 1979). These ambivalent feelings may be upsetting to a child, who then feels guilty at not being as pleased about the remarriage as the parent and stepparent expected (Sager et al., 1983).

Stepchildren sometimes feel unwanted in the stepfamily (Bitterman, 1967). They may feel like the stepparent does not want them around or they may feel like a "fifth wheel" amidst the marital couple's joy. Unfamiliar household rules could lead to a child feeling like an outsider in the family.

Identity confusion is another possible response (Sager et al., 1983). This is, in fact, not a problem only for children but for all family members (Sager, et al., 1983). The absence of societal guidelines for stepfamily roles and the lack of models for stepfamily functioning can cause this identity confusion (Goldner, 1982).

Stress in general can also be a problem for stepchildren (Lutz, 1983). In addition to the daily hassles and stressors that all children face, stepchildren may experience stressors related to adjusting to new family situations, dealing with their more complicated families, or any of the events previously mentioned in this chapter.

Stepfamily Expectations. Inappropriate expectations, erroneous expectations, or those that are unrealistically high, can lead to disenchantment, frustration, unhappiness, and disappointment. Remarried parents, and sometimes their children as well, may be prone to hold inappropriate expectations for their stepfamily lives (Visher & Visher, 1982).

Probably the most common erroneous expectation is that stepfamilies are just like first families (Messinger & Walker, 1981). This is, in the eyes of many stepfamily experts, the most damaging expectation (Visher & Visher, 1979). Those who hold this belief often find out how different their stepfamily is from what they expected. Different family histories, different rules and roles, the existence of biological parents elsewhere, children residing in two households, financial issues, legal issues, names, and potentially most areas of stepfamily life create barriers to the fantasy that stepfamilies are the same as nuclear families (Visher & Visher, 1979). Yet many people attempt to ignore or deny such differences exist; parents especially encourage this by wanting children to act "as if" the stepparent were their biological parent, trying to cut off ties with the "old" extended family, etc. Clinicians often warn that children are less able and willing to do this than parents. This push to re-create the nuclear family can cause stress for children.

Another inappropriate expectation, held by the biological parent, is that the stepparent will rescue the family (Crohn, et al., 1982). This may entail expecting them to take charge in disciplining children, resolving financial problems, and replacing the absent parent emotionally for children. Sometimes stepparents also hold this expectation and sometimes they are successful in fulfilling them. Success is likely, however, only when all stepfamily members want and work for this goal.

Another widely held expectation is that enough love will conquer all problems. "If we love each other enough, things will work out" is a common version of this (Coleman & Ganong, 1985). This expectation can lead to pseudomutuality (ignoring true disagreements), doubts, avoidance of constructive problem-solving and other dysfunctional behavior (Sager, et al., 1981). Another unrealistic expectation about love, that stepparents and stepchildren will love each other instantly, also causes discomfort among stepfamilies (Messinger & Walker, 1981). Love usually take time to grow, and if time to develop love is not allowed, then the "myth of instant love" can result in other effects — stepparents and children may feel guilty about not loving each other, they may pretend and feel dishonest, they may avoid each other because the expectation makes them uncomfortable, or they may dislike each other as a reaction.

Not all troublesome expectations originate within the stepfamily. The negative societal image of stepfamilies can cause stress also. In our culture the term stepchild is used as a synonym for someone or something that is abused, neglected, or unwanted (Coleman & Ganong, 1987).

Fairy tales portray stepchildren as victims, stepmothers as wicked oppressors, and fathers as passive bystanders. Studies have found that the roles of stepmother and stepfather are seen more negatively than other family roles (Fine, 1986; Ganong & Coleman, 1983) and that stereotypes about stepparents (Bryan, Ganong, Coleman & Bryan, 1985; Bryan, Coleman, Ganong & Bryan, 1986) stepchildren (Bryan, et al., 1985; Bryan, et al., 1986), and stepfamilies (Bryant, Coleman & Ganong, 1987) are more negative than stereotypes of other families or family positions. Negative cultural stereotypes influence teachers, clergy, neighbors, and others who may encounter stepfamily members.

Stepfamily members are the pioneers of family living in the final quarter of the twentieth century. The rapid increase in the number of stepfamilies has caught helping professionals, social science researchers, and legal experts poorly prepared to deal with the complex demands of this family form. Although in recent years society has struggled to "catch up" with stepfamilies, members of such families still lack clear cultural role guidelines, still encounter clergy, counselors, and educators who are ignorant of their unique dynamics, and still find themselves on the frontier of constructing strategies for successful stepfamily living.

Those stepfamily members who have turned to counselors and other helping professionals have likely found them to reflect the same general biases and stereotypes held by the broader society (Bryan, Ganong, Coleman, & Bryan, 1985). If they have turned to self-help literature they may have been overwhelmed by the pervasive problem-filled orientation of most of these books. Adults are less likely to read adolescent fiction, but this much larger body of work may be the best source of insightful information about the many conflicting emotions, undercurrents, and general dynamics of stepfamily living. Stepfamily members will quickly know the problems involved in blending families. They need problem-solving strategies and surprisingly few of the self-help books offer comprehensive strategies for dealing with problems. But perhaps most of all, stepfamilies need hope. They need to have access to well-trained counselors and other professionals who understand stepfamily dynamics and who can offer help and hope. They need to be exposed to books that enlighten and expand possibilities rather than focusing on pitfalls and problems. They need to be able to read literature that presents the stepfamily as normal and able to cope with pressures and miscommunication. They need hope as they go about forging new norms for family living in this nation. We can not afford to have such a large proportion of our population so poorly understood. Bulwer-

Lytton (1839) said "The pen is mightier than the sword." Too many step-families have fallen on the sword and disbanded because they didn't un-derstand the dynamics of their own families. The pen has traditionally merely described the many ways stepfamilies can fall on the sword. In Chapter 2 we will describe how literature can be used in a positive way to help stepfamilies.

References

Ahrons, C. R., & Perlmutter, M. S. (1982). The relationship between former spouses: A fundamental subsystem in the remarriage family. In L. Messinger (Ed.), *Therapy with remarried families.* Rockville, MD: Aspen.

Bachrach, C. A. (1983). Children in families: Characteristics of biological, step-, and adopted children. *Journal of Marriage and the Family, 45,* 171-179.

Bitterman, C. (1968). The multimarriage family. *Social Casework, 49,* 218-221.

Bryan, L., Coleman, M., Ganong, L., & Bryan, S. (1986). Person perception: Fam-ily structure as a cue for stereotyping *Journal of Marriage and the Family, 48,* 169-174.

Bryan, H., Ganong, L., Coleman, M., & Bryan, L. (1985). Counselors' perceptions of stepparents and stepchildren. *Journal of Counseling Psychology, 32,* 279-282.

Bryant, L., Coleman, M., & Ganong, L. (in review). Race and family structure ster-eotyping: Perceptions of black and white nuclear families and stepfamilies.

Bumpass, L. (1984). Some characteristics of children's second families. *American Journal of Sociology, 90,* 608-623.

Cherlin, A., & McCarthy, J. (1985). Remarried couple households: Data from the June 1980 current population survey. *Journal of Marriage and the Family, 47,* 23-30.

Cherlin, A. (1978). Remarriage as an incomplete institution. *American Journal of So-ciology, 84,* 634-650.

Coleman, M., & Ganong, L. (1985). Remarriage myths: Implications for the help-ing professions. *Journal of Counseling & Development, 64,* 116-120.

Coleman, M., & Ganong, L. (1987). The cultural stereotyping of stepfamilies. In K. Pasley & M. Ihinger-Tallman (Eds.) *Remarriage and stepparenting: Current research and theory* (pp. 19-41). New York: Guilford.

Crohn, H., Sager, C., Brown, H., Rodstein, E., & Walker, L. (1982). A basis for un-derstanding and treating the remarried family. *Family Therapy Collections, 2,* 159-186.

Fast, I., & Cain, A. C. (1966). The stepparent role: Potential for disturbances in family functioning. *American Journal of Orthopsychiatry, 36,* 485-491.

Fine, M. A. (1986). Perceptions of stepparents: Variation in stereotypes as a function of current family structure. *Journal of Marriage and the Family, 48,* 537-543.

Fishman, B., & Hamel, B. (1981). From nuclear to stepfamily ideology: A stressful change. *Alternative Lifestyles, 4,* 181-204.

Friedman, L. J. (1981). Common problems in stepfamilies. In A. S. Gurman (Ed.), *Questions and answers in the practice of family therapy* (pp. 329-332). New York: Brunner/Mazel.

Ganong, L., & Coleman, M. (1983). Stepparent: A pejorative term? *Psychological Reports, 52,* 919-922.

Ganong, L., & Coleman, M. (1984). Effects of remarriage on children: A review of the empirical literature. *Family Relations, 33,* 389-406.

Ganong, L., & Coleman, M. (1986). A comparison of clinical and empirical literature on children in stepfamilies. *Journal of Marriage and the Family, 48,* 309-318.

Gardner, R. A. (1984). Counseling children in stepfamilies. *Elementary School Guidance and Counseling, 19,* 40-49.

Glick, P. C. (1984). Marriage, divorce and living arrangements: Prospective changes. *Journal of Family Issues, 5,* 7-26.

Goldner, V. (1982). Remarriage family: Structure, system, future. In J. C. Hansen & L. Messenger (Eds.), *Therapy with remarried families* (pp. 187-206). Rockville, MD: Aspen.

Greif, J. B. (1982). The father-child relationship subsequent to divorce. In J. C. Hansen & L. Messenger (Eds.), *Therapy with remarried families* (pp. 47-57). Rockville, MD: Aspen.

Isaacs, M. B. (1982). Facilitating family restructuring and relinkage. In J. C. Hansen & L. Messenger (Eds.), *Therapy with remarried families* (pp. 121-143). Rockville, MD: Aspen.

Jacobson, D. S. (1984, April). *Family type, visiting, and children's behavior in the stepfamily: A linked family system.* Paper presented at the annual meeting of the American Orthopsychiatric Association, Toronto, Ontario.

Jones, S. M. (1978). Divorce and remarriage: A new beginning, a new set of problems. *Journal of Divorce, 2,* 217-227.

Kompara, D. R. (1980). Difficulties in the socialization of stepparenting. *Family Relations, 29,* 69-73.

Lutz, P. (1983). The stepfamily: An adolescent perspective. *Family Relations, 32,* 367-376.

Maddox, B. (1975). *The half parent: Living with other people's children.* NY: New American Library.

McGoldrick, M., & Carter, E. A. (1980). Forming a remarried family. In E. A. Carter & M. McGoldrick (Eds.), *The family cycle: A framework for family therapy* (pp. 265-294). NY: Gardner Press.

Messinger, L. (1984). *Remarriage: A family affair.* NY: Plenum.

Messinger, L., & Walker, K. (1981). From marriage breakdown to remarriage: Parental tasks and therapeutic guidelines. *American Journal of Orthopsychiatry, 51,* 429-438.

Mowatt, M. (1972). Group psychotherapy for stepfathers and their wives. *Psychotherapy: Theory, Research and Practice, 9,* 328-331.

Podolsky, E. (1955). The emotional problems of the stepchild. *Mental Hygiene, 39,* 49-53.

Sager, C. J., Brown, H. S., Crohn, H., Engel, T., Rodstein, E., & Walker, E. (1983). *Treating the remarried family.* NY: Brunner/Mazel.

Sager, C. J., Walker, E., Brown, H. S., Crohn, H., & Rodstein, E. (1981). Improving function of the remarried family system. *Journal of Marital and Family Therapy,* Jan., 3-13.

Stanton, G. W. (1986). Preventive intervention with stepfamilies. *Social Work, 31,* 201-206.

Visher, E. B., & Visher, J. S. (1979). *Stepfamilies: A guide to working with stepparents and stepchildren.* NY: Brunner/Mazel.

Wald, E. (1981). *The remarried family: Challenge and promise.* NY: Family Service Association of America.

Walker, K. N., & Messenger, L. (1979). Remarriage after divorce: Dissolution and reconstruction of family boundaries. *Family Process, 18,* 185-192.

Whiteside, M. F. (1981). A family systems approach with families of remarriage. In I. R. Stuart & L. E. Abt (Eds.), *Children of separation and divorce.* NY: Van Nostrand Reinhold.

Whiteside, M. F. (1982). Remarriage: A family developmental process. *Journal of Marital and Family Therapy, 4,* 59-68.

Whiteside, M. F. (1983). Families of remarriage: The weaving of many life cycle threads. *Family Therapy Collections, 7,* 100-119.

CHAPTER 2

THE USES OF FICTION
AND SELF-HELP BOOKS WITH CHILDREN
AND ADOLESCENTS IN STEPFAMILIES

IN THIS AGE of electronic media it is still likely to be books that hook the imagination of children and adolescents. Only through books can the reader completely escape into new roles and identities and sample lives and lifestyles vicariously. Good fiction often provides children and adolescents with models to help them handle situations they might encounter. Good nonfiction (e.g., self-help books) provides children and adolescents with concrete advice and suggestions to help them better handle situations. Both types of books can be important aids to educators, counselors, and other helping professionals working with children and adolescents living in stepfamilies.

One technique for using these books with young people is bibliotherapy. Bibliotherapy has been known by many names, such as bibliocounseling, bibliopsychology, biblioeducation, biblioguidance, library therapeutics, biblioprophylaxis, tutorial group therapy, and literotherapy (Rubin, 1978). Bibliotherapy has been defined as "guidance in the solution of personal problems through directed reading" (Webster, 1981) and "a family of techniques for structuring an interaction between a facilitator and a participant . . . based on their mutual sharing of literature" (Berry, 1978). In the last half century bibliotherapy increasingly has been used in noninstitutional settings (e.g., schools, private and public mental health agencies, and private practices) by a variety of professionals including counselors, social workers, psychologists, nurses, psychiatrists, ministers, and educators. Although training in bibliotherapy has been encouraged (Rubin, 1978), most helping professionals who use the technique have had minimal preparation, if any.

Bibliotherapy may be done with groups or individuals. Berry (1978) has identified two types of bibliotherapy, clinical and educational/ humanistic. Clinical bibliotherapy is used mostly within a context of counseling or therapy with individuals who have emotional or behavioral problems that are relatively disabling (Shrank & Engels, 1981).

Educational bibliotherapy is most appropriate when dealing with developmental problems or minor adjustment problems. For most helping professionals wishing to incorporate bibliotherapy into their practice, educational bibliotherapy is most practical to consider (Baruth & Burggraf, 1984). Educational bibliotherapy can be used as a preventive technique or as a method to help clients handle already-existing difficulties. Although empirical evidence is sparse, there is some research with children that has found bibliotherapy to be effective in changing attitudes (S. M. Agnes, 1947; Fisher, 1968) and in enhancing personal and social adjustment (Heminghaus, 1954). For some populations, educational bibliotherapy may be either a valuable adjunct to counseling or an alternative (Baruth & Phillips, 1976; Cianciolo, 1965; McInnes, 1982; McKinney, 1977).

The purposes of educational bibliotherapy are diverse: (1) to impart information, (2) to provide insight, (3) to stimulate discussion about problems, (4) to communicate new attitudes and values, (5) to create awareness that others have similar problems, (6) to teach new solutions to problems, (7) to enhance self-esteem, and (8) to furnish relaxation and diversion (Baruth & Burggraf, 1984; Cianciolo, 1965; Griffin, 1984; McKinney, 1977; Zaccaria & Moses, 1968). The first three goals are perhaps the most important.

Through the use of assigned and shared reading a variety of information can be conveyed, including new facts, different ways of approaching problems, and alternative ways of thinking about problems (Griffin, 1984). This function of bibliotherapy may be particularly helpful to stepfamily members, since most of them have limited prior knowledge or personal experience with stepfamily functioning. In fact, many clinicians assert that unrealistic expectations and expectations based on nuclear family models create many difficulties for stepfamily members (Mills, 1984; Papernow, 1984; Visher & Visher, 1979). Bibliotherapy is a helpful method of informing stepchildren and their parents about step-relationships and the unique challenges they may encounter.

Insight, or self-understanding, is another major goal of bibliotherapy (Baruth & Burggraf, 1984; Cianciolo, 1965; McKinney, 1977; Schultheis, 1972; Zaccaria & Moses, 1968). In reading about a character who is facing a situation similar to their own, readers may identify with the character and in so doing may gain some awareness and understanding of their own motivations, thoughts, and feelings (Griffin, 1984). By reading about a book character's conflicts, emotional reactions and cognitions, a reader can better realize their own reactions and thoughts. Readers may also gain understanding of situations they might be facing, such as having stepsiblings or visiting a noncustodial parent and stepparent (Hynes & Hynes-Berry, 1986; Zaccaria & Moses, 1968). Greater understanding of other people may be another benefit of bibliotherapy (Cianciolo, 1965; McKinney, 1977). A greater appreciation of the motives and feelings of characters that represent persons in the life of a stepchild (e.g., a stepfather, a mother) may result.

The third major purpose, to stimulate discussion, is useful when topics may not otherwise be openly discussed because of fear, guilt, or shame (McKinney, 1977). Reading about a character who has to handle similar stepfamily issues may help a young reader realize that others face the same issues and situations and may help impart a sense of normality that otherwise might be absent. Embarrassment over parental divorce and remarriage is a problem to some children and adolescents (Visher & Visher, 1979). Social stigma over "step" status may discourage children from openly sharing their good and bad family experiences with others (Coleman & Ganong, 1987). Sometimes, the sheer complexity of stepfamily living encourages stepchildren to control the amount of disclosing they do. As a young friend told us, "I used to talk about my stepfamily more often, but when I start to describe where everyone lives and the half- and steprelationships, people's eyes glaze over and I can tell they haven't a clue about what I am talking about." Bibliotherapy as a discussion stimulant may be particularly useful with stepchildren.

When most professionals think of bibliotherapy they think of giving clients self-help books or pamphlets of practical advice or information. However, educational bibliotherapy can also include the use of assigned fictional readings.

Choosing Fiction

Selecting novels for use in biblioeducation is not necessarily an easy task. Some readers enjoy mysteries, some prefer science fiction, others would choose an adventure story. Biblioeducation has been found to work best when children are allowed to choose their own reading (Hynes

& Hynes-Berry, 1986). This does not mean that children should be free to read anything they want; rather, professional helpers should present readers with choices from a limited, carefully chosen selection (Jalongo, 1983).

Several criteria have been identified for selecting books for stepchildren:

a. the stepfamily issues should be the main focus,
b. the book should be at the child's reading level,
c. the stories should be about modern children or have universal appeal,
d. characters should be realistic and the solutions to problems should be realistic,
e. materials should not offend religious beliefs or values of the reader (McInnes, 1982).

To this list of criteria should be added:

f. the book should have literary merit,
g. problems should be dealt with in a manner consistent with research or prevailing clinical opinion about stepfamily functioning,
h. good coping strategies should be presented in the books.

It would be pointless for the stepchild to read about ineffective coping techniques unless good coping techniques are presented as well. A related issue is the way crises are presented. Crises should be presented in an optimistic, surmountable fashion. The point of bibliotherapy is not to leave the reader despairing and depressed. Ideally, the books will present new options and solutions to problems. Books cannot be chosen until the stepchild's situation is known. Structural characteristics of the family such as the number of siblings, stepsiblings, and half-siblings, the cause of dissolution of parents' marriage (death or divorce), and extent of contact with the non-residential parent should be considered as part of the family situation. Of course, the presenting problem or issues of concern also should be part of the selection process.

It is important that quality not be sacrificed for relevance. When an area becomes "hot," books for children on that topic often flood the market. Though the books may relate to a currently relevant topic, many are poorly written and uninteresting. If a book doesn't qualify as good literature it should not be used with children.

For some purposes, books that feature stepchildren in roles incidental to the story as well as those in which the stepfamily situation is central to the plot, could be used. Children and adults, whether in stepfamilies or not, might benefit from seeing step status treated in a normative fashion (i.e., having a stepfather regarded as no big deal). Certainly school librarians and educators should want to have some of these "incidental" books in their collections. Books with secondary or incidental stepfamily themes may have other themes that are relevant to the child and his or her family. If the child appears resistant to reading stepfamily literature, some of the other books may be used to gradually move him or her into discussing stepfamily dynamics.

Once the stepchild's situation is known, and a book is selected, the book should then be read by the clinician/educator. Questions to ask when reading include: Can the child relate to the main character and to the story?; Is the book written at the child's reading level?; Is the story realistic and relevant?. If answers to these questions are "yes," then the book could be presented to the child.

How to Use Fiction

Jalongo (1983) has outlined a relatively simple four-step process for using fiction in bibliotherapy.

1. Plan. This includes identification of the individual's needs and selection of appropriate material. Planning demands that the helper know the child, at least some information about the family, and the reading material.

Jalongo (1983) suggests that questions be prepared at this stage. Questions may be presented to the reader prior to reading, interspersed throughout the reading experience, and/or at the conclusion of reading. Questions should be designed to improve the quality of the reading experience by, for example, focusing the reader's attention, eliciting certain thoughts and feelings, stimulating thinking about solutions, and encouraging the identification process. Questions that encourage the reader to analyze characters' behavior, apply information to their own experience, and synthesize coping and problem-solving techniques are appropriate as well.

2. Motivate. The introduction of material and the presentation of the reading experience is extremely important (Griffin, 1984; Jalongo, 1983). It is not useful to simply suggest that a book be read. Introductory comments should be designed to encourage the child to want to read the book. Comments such as, "You know, a boy in this book had a family situation pretty much like yours. It might be interesting for you to read this, just to see how he handled it. We could talk about it afterwards and think of ways the story could have been different," might serve as motivation.

At this stage, the reader may be told about what will be done following reading the book. This can range among: (a) summarizing and discussing the story, (b) talking about alternative endings, (c) discussing what the reader would have done in the protagonists' place, (d) imagining how the story might have been told from the perspective of the stepparent, a sibling, or a parent, (e) discussing how certain incidents in the story may have affected subsequent events, (f) discussing parallels between the story and the reader's life. Whatever is planned, this should be explained in a way that encourages and motivates the child.

3. Present. This is the stage of shared reading. It may include asking questions and responding with answers to children's comments and concerns.

4. Follow-up. This is an important step that should not be missed (Baruth & Burggraf, 1984; Griffin, 1984; Jalongo, 1983). Follow-up can be a discussion based on previously prepared questions or it could take whatever format has been decided upon. This is a time to clarify any information presented in the books, review concepts, evaluate the story or characters in the story, and explore children's feelings. Some children may need assistance in summarizing and evaluating reading material. Other children may need help in exploring their own attitudes and feelings.

Ciancialo (1965) suggests that follow-up should include several activities. There should be a retelling of the story. The incidents, feelings, and relationships that are relevant should be discussed. Analyzing these in depth can facilitate the child's identification with the books' characters. Attempts should be made to identify similar incidents in the experience of the reader. The reader should be encouraged to explore the consequences of certain behaviors or feelings. The reader is also encouraged to determine the desirability or helpfulness of several alternatives.

In addition to discussing alternative endings and analyzing the thoughts, feelings, and behaviors of the book characters (and discussing alternative thoughts, feelings, and behaviors), the following activities can be part of the follow-up stage:

1. Have the child fantasize about what the main character will be doing, thinking, and feeling in a year following the book's end and 5 years later? This same kind of activity can be done for other characters in the book as well.

2. If the story has been written from the main character's point of view (and most are), a discussion of the events of the story from the viewpoint of other characters might be helpful in encouraging the reader to understand and appreciate other perspectives. If the fiction is presented from the stepchild's view, a retelling of the story from the stepfather or mother's view might be insightful for the child.

3. Discuss possible advantages to the family situation that the main character did not consider. It is important to identify positive or potentially positive aspects of stepfamily living; often advantages or resources are unused if stepchildren are not aware of them.

4. Role play scenes from the story. Alternative outcomes may be role played, the child may be asked to play the role of several characters in the book, and other variations to the role play can be introduced. This method lends itself to group settings but it can also be done with dyads.

5. Have the reader play "Dear Abby" with the main characters. Write a Dear Abby letter based on the story and have the reader verbally respond or write out a helpful answer.

6. Younger children may enjoy drawing scenes or stories from the book. These drawings can be used to facilitate an exploration of the thoughts and feelings experienced by characters in the story.

Whatever the follow-up activity entails, it is important that the helper respond nonjudgementally to reader's comments. Patience is a virtue; some readers may benefit from bibliotherapy but may have a difficult time disclosing thoughts and feelings.

Using Juvenile Fiction With Adults

It should be noted that fiction written for children and adolescents can also be used effectively with adults. A well-written, honestly portrayed stepfamily story can be informative and instructional for adult readers. Young reader fiction can be read quickly by adults of average or above-average reading ability and even adults who read poorly can handle this literature. Since most of these books are told from the child's perspective, adult readers cannot avoid being exposed to how their stepchildren or children might be experiencing their family. The previously mentioned activities can be effectively employed with adults as well as children.

Remarried parents and stepparents can benefit from reading juvenile fiction, especially adolescent novels, nearly as much as their children do.

Fiction could serve as a catalyst for dialogue and discussion in stepfamily educational programs; both adults and children could engage in discussion activities following the shared reading of a work of fiction. Children could role play adults portrayed in the story and adults could act as the child main characters. Families could together plan the future of book characters, or draw a picture together, or write their own short story about a fictional stepfamily.

Juvenile fiction could also be assigned reading to adults who are planning to remarry as part of premarriage preparation. For some adults, reading about a fictional stepfamily is more comfortable than critically analyzing one's own situation and may provide a safe arena for examining potential difficulties.

Because adolescent fiction tends to be well-written and concise, a great deal of it can be read in a relatively short period of time. Parents can learn a great deal about their children and children in general from reading fiction targeted toward young people. Adolescent fiction can provide insight into the passions, problems, and concerns of children undergoing change. Adolescents reading fiction may find their situation is not so bad after all, or they may learn new ways of coping with their changing life. They may also develop empathy with their parents and insight into how children's behavior can destroy families and harm the child in the process. For families who are not skilled in sharing feelings, the fact that everyone in the family is reading the same books may be a first step in communication. Families might also benefit from discussing the characters in the book and the plot, a less threatening activity than discussing their own personal feelings. Other families might benefit from lively discussion of the books, applying it to themselves and other family members, and deciding on the realism or lack of realism in the presentation of the fictional stepfamilies. Perceptive parents can ask, "Have you ever felt like _____ (book character)?" or "I don't see how the _____ family survived with all the problems they had. Does our household ever seem like that to you?"

Fiction can be a powerful tool of understanding within any family. The advantage of adolescent or children's fiction for shared family reading experience is it's clarity and brevity. More books can be shared in a short period of time. Since family life, especially stepfamily life, is complex, it is helpful to read widely and find out about families from as many perspectives as possible. Books have always unlocked doors of the mind, and they have the potential of providing a key to understanding the rapidly growing phenomena known as the modern American stepfamily.

We have also assigned young reader fiction to graduate students studying stepfamily dynamics, as a way to quickly expose them to the complexities of step living. It has been our experience that reading several of the highly recommended books for adolescents "brings home" the realities of stepfamily living to students in a way that reading in professional journals and books do not. In a way, the fiction is used as an alternative to reading case studies.

Although the students in our stepfamily course are graduate students studying psychology, child development, social work, or nursing, the same purposes can be achieved with non-stepfamily adult and child readers. Reading realistic, quality fiction about stepfamily living can be helpful in aiding others' understanding of some of the issues faced by stepchildren and their parents. Even though, as a rule, juvenile fiction does not portray all the real-life complexity of many stepfamilies, readers who are not in stepfamilies are less likely to have their eyes "glaze over" with confusion when they later encounter a real stepfamily.

Using Stepfamily Fiction With Children From Other Families

We have mentioned some benefits for non-stepfamily members already; gaining understanding and appreciation of a different family form. Stigma associated with step status can be reduced and tolerance for different ways of living in a family can be increased by reading quality fiction about stepchildren. Reading fiction could also serve as part of a child's preparation for parental remarriage.

Choosing Self-Help Books

Choosing self-help books for children and adolescents is relatively easy compared to selecting fiction. One reason is that the universe of available books is small. An exhaustive search of the literature produced only 12 self-help books for stepchildren: 2 for adolescents, 3 for young adolescents or older children, and 7 for children.

Several criteria need to be considered in selecting self-help books for children and adolescents. First of all, as with fiction, self-help material needs to be well matched to the child's reading ability. A self-help book that is too difficult for the child will not be read. Recommending a book that is too simple will be found insulting and may damage rapport between the child and the educator or counselor. It is also probably a waste of time to give a child who seldom reads a self-help book as adjunct to counseling. Xeroxed sections of books relating specifically to the child's problems might be attempted for the nonreader. Whether the child is a voracious reader or one who is only likely to respond to one page a month, it is imperative that the material be discussed with the child. In some cases reading alone is sufficient therapy, but these cases are the exception (Zaccaria & Moses, 1968).

A second point to consider when making a self-help book selection is the number of issues and problems discussed. We have found, in general, that the more issues dealt with, the better the overall quality of the book (Coleman & Ganong, 1987). Some children may be more willing to discuss their problems after reading a self-help book that parallels their experiences. The books can also create awareness that others have similar problems. This may lessen the sense of isolation that's not uncommon to stepchildren. Those books that place at least minimal emphasis on strengths in stepfamilies can teach positive and constructive thinking.

A third factor is the quantity and quality of advice given. Advice for children needs to be clear and concrete to be effective (Piaget, 1973). For example, specific ideas on how to word questions and statements, such as "Do I have to love her [stepmother]?" and "I want you [biological mother] to spend more time with me" is better advice (more concrete) than admonitions to "communicate feelings." If advice is to be useful it must be within the abilities of most children.

A fourth area to consider is the number of strengths of stepfamily living depicted in the book. A well-balanced perspective is important. If only problems in stepfamilies are presented, the message conveyed to the child is that living in a stepfamily is a totally negative situation.

The fifth aspect to consider in selecting self-help books is the "extras" such as illustrations, prefaces for biological parents and stepparents, reference lists, helpful appendices, and the overall visual appeal of the book. In general, good children's self-help books will also appeal to adults, and it's probably advisable that the whole family read and discuss the book. Illustrations should be attractive and represent diverse racial and ethnic groups. Younger children are more attracted to highly colorful illustrations. Prefaces and afterwords for adults enhance the appeal and the usefulness of the book. Such "extras" facilitate full family participation and discussion. Reference lists of classic or recent books can be of great value to the reader wishing to discover more about the subject. Lists of appropriate stepfamily fiction would be appreciated by many motivated readers. Thorough appendices can expand the usefulness of a self-help book. Such appendices might contain addresses of stepfamily organizations, phone numbers for crisis hotlines, sources of helping professionals, etc. Though the overall visual appeal of the book is listed as an "extra," only a veteran reader is likely to tackle a book that is not well designed. Small print, tightly compacted pages, and page layouts lacking in visual interest are turnoffs to most child and adolescent readers.

The sixth and final characteristic to consider is the tone of the book. The author should use a nonjudgmental tone and not be condescending to the reader. The use of humor is a valuable quality in self-help books.

How to Use Self-Help Books

Although most advice or self-help books are written for adult readers, in recent years authors of such works have written for children and adolescents as well. If carefully chosen, some of the material may be used effectively for specific purposes.

For example, self-help books may be used for conveying advice to stepchildren on ways to think, act, and cope with problems. Sometimes reading advice is preferable to children than to be told the same advice by a counselor or parent; reading allows more time for children to consider the merits of the advice, and it removes some of the potential for power struggles that may result in children rejecting the advice just because of the source. A helping professional may suggest a particular reading selection if they suspect that the same advice from them would evoke rejection of the ideas.

Self-help books often contain structured activities that children can do. These activities may be designed to encourage problem-solving, to stimulate communication with parents and stepparents, or to help children identify and process their feelings. These activities can be assigned as homework in therapy, as part of group activities in educational groups, or they can be done with the helping professional serving as the "parent."

Self-help books also can be used to stimulate role-playing. Children can role-play action described in the books or they can demonstrate alternative ways of responding to certain situations. Children can be asked to imagine how parents and stepparents would react to the child if the book's advice were followed. After reading a self-help book children could brainstorm alternatives from what was read, such as other ways of dealing with the events portrayed or other strengths not mentioned.

It should be noted that self-help books are not for the stepchild having severe emotional problems. The books are designed to educate the child about stepfamily living and to provide insight to the child having mild to moderate problems in adjusting to stepfamily living. They also, in some cases, provide information that may help a child avoid problems in the future.

Bibliotherapy is not a panacea for stepchildren. Stepfamily fiction and self-help books will not undo the complexity of stepfamily living. They can, however, in conjunction with counseling, provide children with a wealth of advice, general information, and guidelines to try out as they adjust to their new status.

References

Agnes, S. (1947). The influence of reading in the racial attitudes of adolescent girls. *The Catholic Educational Review, 45,* 415-420.

Baruth, L. & Burggraf, M. (1984). The counselor and single-parent families. *Elementary School Guidance and Counseling, 19,* 30-37.

Baruth, L. & Phillips, M. (1976). Bibliotherapy and the school counselor. *School Counselor, 23,* 191-199.

Berry, I. (1978). Contemporary bibliotherapy: Systematizing the field. In E. J. Rubin (Ed.), *Bibliotherapy Sourcebook* (pp. 185-190). Phoenix, AZ: Oryx Press.

Cianciolo, P. (1965). Children's literature can affect coping behavior. *Personnel and Guidance Journal, 44,* 897-903.

Coleman, M. & Ganong, L. (1987). The cultural stereotyping of stepfamilies. In K. Pasley & M. Ihinger-Tallman (Eds.), *Remarriage and stepparenting: Current research and theory.* (pp. 19-41). New York: Guilford.

Fisher, F. (1968). Influence of reading and discussion on attitudes of fifth graders toward American Indians. *Journal of Educational Research, 62,* 130-134.

Griffin, B. (1984). *Special needs bibliography: Current books for/about children and young adults.* DeWitt, NY: Griffin.

Heminghaus, E. (1954). *The effect of bibliotherapy on the attitudes and personal and social adjustment of a group of elementary school children.* Unpublished doctoral dissertation, Washington University. Dissertation Abstracts International 14, 1641.

Hynes, A. & Hynes-Berry, M. (1986). *Bibliotherapy - The interactive process: A handbook.* Boulder, CO: Westview.

Jalongo, M. (1983). Using crisis-oriented books with young children. *Young Children, 39,* 29-36.

McInnes, K. (1982). Bibliotherapy: Adjunct to traditional counseling with children of stepfamilies. *Child Welfare, 61,* 153-160.

McKinney, F. (1977). Exploration in bibliotherapy. *Personnel and Guidance Journal, 56,* 550-552.

Mills, D. (1984). A model for stepfamily development. *Family Relations, 33,* 365-372.

Papernow, P. (1984). The stepfamily cycle: An experimental model of stepfamily development. *Family Relations, 33,* 355-364.

Piaget, J. (1973). *Language and thoughts of the child.* New York: World.

Rubin, R. (1978). *Using bibliotherapy: A guide to theory and practice.* Phoenix, AR: Oryx Press.

Schrank, F. & Engels, D. (1981). Bibliotherapy as a counseling adjunct: Research findings. *Personnel and Guidance Journal, 60,* 143-147.

Schultheis, M. (1972). *A guidebook for bibliotherapy.* Glenview, IL: Psychotechnics.

Visher, E. & Visher, J. (1979). *Stepfamilies: A guide to working with stepparents and stepchildren.* NY: Brunner/Mazel.

Webster's New Collegiate Dictionary. (1981). Springfield, MA: Merriam-Webster.

Zaccaria, J. & Moses, H. (1968). *Facilitating human development through reading: The use of bibliotherapy in teaching and counseling.* Champaign, IL: Stipes.

CHAPTER 3

REVIEWING STEPFAMILY FICTION BOOKS FOR CHILDREN AND ADOLESCENTS

FINDING BOOKS about stepchildren and stepfamilies is not difficult; they are in every library and bookstore in North America. Our goal was to be as thorough as possible in reading and reviewing all the available books, however, and so our search procedures were designed to cast as wide a net as possible. In this chapter we will describe the sampling methods used to locate the fiction and self-help books. In addition, the methods of reviewing will be described and the process of critiquing and assessing the quality of the books will be explained.

Locating Stepfamily Fiction

An exhaustive search was conducted. We started by looking for books in the standard reference works. There are a number of publications that list children's books; we examined a decade's worth of such resources. The stepfamily fiction for children derived from these references became the "foundation" of our sample. Altogether, a dozen reference works were employed in the search:

1. School Library Journal
2. Publishers Weekly
3. The Hornbook
4. Booklist
5. Bulletins for the Center of Children's Books
6. The Elementary School Library Collection (Winkel, 1982; 1986)
7. The Bookfinder, Vols. 1, 2 & 3 (Dreyer, 1977, 1981)
8. Book company catalogues
9. Subject Guide to Children's Books in Print (Bowker, 1981; 1985; 1987-88)

10. Best Books for Children: Preschool (Gillespie & Gilbert, 1981; 1985)
11. Children's Books in Print 1985-1986 (Bowker, 1985; 1987-88)
12. Helping Children Cope With Separation and Loss (Bernstein, 1983).

In addition, we used standard search procedures, such as looking in card catalogs in several libraries and asking librarians for references they knew of. Other sources for books included libraries of acquaintances, publishing company catalogs, newspaper book reviews, retail bookstores, and bookstores specializing in used books. Students, friends, and colleagues were quite helpful in telling us about the fiction they found.

Every book identified from the sources just mentioned were reviewed. Many publishers provided us with copies and the University of Missouri Library helped us gather many books through the inter-library loan system.

Reviewing the Fiction

Every book was read and evaluated by at least one of us, and half were read by one of us and one other person. In some cases the second reader was Dr. Susan Marshall Roberts, a reading specialist with an interest in stepfamilies; in some cases it was a trained graduate student in child development; and in some cases we served as checks for each other.

For determining the quality of the stepfamily fiction a 1-5 scale developed by Dr. Susan Marshall Roberts was used.

Literary Quality Scale

1 = "No Merit"
• Little depth to the characters
• May be some plot but plot is very unclear
• Reader leaves with no better understanding of life or with a distorted view of life
• Filled with gimmicks to attract and tantalize the reader in a "common sort of way" (i.e., "offensive," "shocking," or "off-color" language; events which are intended to shock; silly, inane, or "bizarre" characters)

2 = "Some Merit"
• Main character(s) is(are) somewhat developed
• A plot of some sort is present; book is designed to entertain alone
• Little or no theme or direction of the reader toward understanding
• Gimmicks, if present, are at a minimum

3 = "Average Merit"

- Some development of most characters
- Fairly good plot; story is not totally predictable; sense of movement
- Author's major purpose is to entertain; however, theme is beginning to emerge

4 = "Above Average"

- Main characters are developed; good sense of thought processes of the character telling the story
- Theme is emerging as the principal aspect of the story with the plot beginning to be used not primarily as a way to entertain but rather to illustrate the theme
- Provides some understanding of life; one has some sense of having read something of value to one's own life

5 = "Superior Merit"

- All (or almost all) characters are well developed (within the limitations of the book)
- The plot serves to illustrate the theme of the story
- The book broadens and sharpens the reader's awareness of life
- A strong sense of having read something of value to one's own life

Obviously, a certain amount of subjectivity occurs when reviewers rate the books. However, over half the books reviewed were coded and critiqued by at least two persons and inter-rater reliability was quite high. Raters were never more than one scale point apart on quality determination.

A criterion for recommending any book was that it be of at least average literary merit. In addition, it was decided that it would be helpful for helping professionals to know:

- the stepfamily structure (i.e., stepmother, stepfather, both)
- if step and half siblings are included in the story
- the reason for the stepfamily formation (i.e., death or divorce in previous family)
- the age and sex of the main character
- a basic plot summary
- whether the stepfamily situation is central, secondary, or incidental to the plot
- suggested age range of readers
- whether or not the book is recommended (from a stepfamily perspective)

Each book was coded accordingly, and the quality rating was determined using the scale for literary merit that we developed. The coded information, including an abbreviated summary and the overall rating, is provided for you in the last section of the book, "Book Summary and Coding." Childrens' picture books and child/adolescent self-help books were evaluated separately. In this chapter the evaluative summaries of the books for preschoolers and young children are presented, followed by summary information of the books for children and adolescents.

Children's Picture Books

And thus began a hard time for the poor stepchild. — Bros. Grimm

Children's picture books should first and foremost be of good literary quality. Literary quality is sometimes overlooked in the rush to provide "relevant" books for newly discovered needs (i.e., books featuring minorities, children from single parent families, females, handicapped children, etc., as the protagonist). For example, some excellent books for preschoolers were published during the late 60's and early 70's featuring minorities (e.g., Ezra Jack Keats' books), but a glut of low quality books have also been marketed.

A related but yet uniquely different situation is that of books about stepfamilies written for preschoolers. Books of excellent literary quality (e.g., Snow White, Cinderella, Little Sister and the Month Brothers) are available, but they present an extremely negative stereotype of stepfamily members and stepfamily living.

Because many people tend to divorce after a short period of marriage and remarry again quite soon, it can be assumed that a sizeable percentage of stepchildren are preschoolers. An even larger percentage of preschoolers in nuclear families today will become stepchildren before their 18th birthday (Glick, 1987). Exposure to Cinderella and Snow White as the models for stepchildren, consistent portrayals of stepmothers as wicked women who treat their biological children preferentially, and stepfathers as ineffectual (but loving) "wimps", is not positive socialization for adjusting to stepfamily living. It's little wonder that reaction to even the term "stepmother" and "stepfather" is relatively negative (Ganong & Coleman, 1983).

The search for preschool books was conducted in the same manner as the other searches with slightly more attention paid to sources such as preschool teachers and parents. Some general observations are in order about the small body of stepfamily literature for young children that was uncovered.

First of all, only one of the authors was male and that was a 12-year-old boy. It is likely due to the over-representation of female authors, that most of the stories are written about stepmothers. However, children are much more likely to live with a stepfather than a stepmother (Cherlin & McCarthy, 1985). There is certainly a place for more good literature reflecting stepfather/stepchild dynamics, however, the two stepfather books that are reviewed are both quite good. Seven of the books centered on noncustodial stepmother/stepchild relationships (the "visiting" child) and a huge population of children fall into this category. The best of these books should be available in every preschool classroom, and teacher training on resourceful ways to use them could be helpful.

Because books for young children are short, fewer themes can be dealt with than in books for older children. For that reason a synopsis of each book is included in this chapter. Another difference between the books for the very young and older children is the importance of pictures for the former. Much of the meaning of a book's content is transferred to preschoolers through the illustrations.

A sizable percentage of the books have Black children as the central characters. This is unfortunately not true of the fiction for older children where the focus is primarily on White middle and upper-middle class children. The preschool books featuring Black children are very well written and have universal appeal with the theme being family centered and the race incidental.

It should be noted that although some of these books are not of high literary quality, a skilled parent or teacher could enhance them or use only portions of the books as impetus to discussion. For the most part these are not books the children themselves will be reading.

1. Boyd, Lizi (1987). *The Not-So-Wicked Stepmother,* New York: Viking Penguin.

   Humorous illustrations by the author add considerably to this story intended to dispel the myth of the wicked stepmother in young children's minds. The examples in the story might be most helpful in explaining visiting stepchildrens' behaviors to unwary stepparents. We're not sure children in the 3-8 year age range the book appears appropriate for would fully understand the dynamics, however. It could probably be used effectively as a counseling tool, however, as a point of departure for discussing feelings and behaviors with a stepchild who visits her father or stepmother.

2. Bunting, Eve (1979). *The Big Red Barn,* New York: Harcourt, Brace, Jovanovich. Illustrations by Howard Knotes.

This book is a companion to *Winter's Coming* which deals with the death of the boy's mother. The big red barn gave him security because it was where he went to cry when his mother died and when his stepmother arrived. The barn burns down one night and the building of the new barn serves as a metaphor for accepting the new stepmother.

"You think we should paint the new barn?" he asked.

"Red paint won't make it be the old barn," I said.

"No," grandpa said. "What's gone's gone. We have to let go of it."

"The new barn's not going to take the old barn's place." I sounded fierce and I felt fierce. Inside me things seemed to be boiling over.

"That's right," grandpa said. "The new barn has to make it's own place. It will if we give it a chance." He sat very still and I couldn't tell when he looked across the field if he was looking at the barn or at Emma.

Beautiful metaphoric story. Children 7 or 8 and above might understand the metaphor but children 3 and up would enjoy the story and illustrations. Enchanting book.

3. Clifton, Lucille (1977). *Everett Anderson's 1-2-3-,* New York: Holt, Rinehart and Winston. Illustrations by Ann Grifalconi.

Everett's mother is considering remarriage and Everett's concerns are presented through the numerals 1 ("a lonely number"), 2 ("I have gotten used to Two"), and 3 ("Three can be crowded or can be just right"). Nice rhymes and simple pleasing illustrations of a Black family. The content is exceptionally impressive considering that it's all in rhyme. Deals with issues and concerns (how things will change for them) very young children are likely to have when a stepfamily is formed.

4. Clifton, Lucille (1978). *Everett Anderson's Nine Month Long,* New York: Holt, Rinehart and Winston. Illustrations by Ann Grifalconi.

Sequel to Everett Anderson's 1-2-3. Wonderful black and white illustrations and positive presentation of a stepfamily through verse. Issues include Everett keeping his last name, love being the important thing, rather than a common name, holding family together, and the arrival of Everett's baby sister.

5. Cooney, Barbara *Little Brother and Little Sister,* Doubleday, Garden City, New York, 1982.

(Preschool through grade 5) Fairy tale, a wicked stepmother who's really a witch; a mean ugly stepsister, a brother who's under a spell (he's a fawn) etc. A romantic, well-written story that unfortunately fosters the wicked stepmother myth.

6. DeRegniers, Beatrice Schnek *Little Sister and the Month Brothers,* A Clarion Book, New York: Seabury Press, 1976.

    A Slavic fairy tale with the age-old wicked stepmother and stepsister who are jealous of "Little Sister." Little Sister's mother and father were both dead so she lived with the stepmother. "This was once upon a time, in the days when stepmothers were wicked and stepsisters were mean and lazy."

    Little Sister had to do all the work and kept getting prettier. Stepmother wanted to get rid of her so that any man who came along would choose her daughter instead of Little Sister, so she was sent on errands (e.g., to find violets in the snow in January). She found the Month brothers and they, of course, helped her. The story presents the typical stereotype of the wicked stepmother.

7. DeWitt, Jamie (1984). *Jamie's Turn,* Milwaukee: Raintree. Illustrations by Julie Brincklae.

    The author describes a true story, how he at age 11 rescued his stepfather after a farm accident with a corn picker. During the next year, while Butch recovered, Jamie did the farm chores. Jamie, a learning disabled child, wrote the book when he was 12. He relates that the incident brought him closer to his stepdad and also made his stepdad proud of him. An inspirational story that would appeal to children aged 4-10.

8. Drescher, Joan (1986). *My Mother's Getting Married,* New York: Dial.

    A colorfully illustrated book for the young reader. Among issues dealt with are the child's concern about how life will be different for her after the remarriage and jealousy and resentment at having to share her mother's time. Realistic portrayal.

9. Green, Phyllis (1975). *Ice River,* Reading, MA: Addison-Wesley. Illustrations by Jim Crowell.

    A sad but well-written story of a boy whose father never visits him ("That was my dad," he said. "He says he'll come on Sunday. Of course he won't come. But he'll want to. That's what's important.") The phone call comes the day Dell almost drowns, thought his dog **had** drowned and his mother had a miscarriage. The stepfather is not a rescuer but is a solid, responsible person who obviously cares for Dell. Realistic dynamics in the story line. The dog returns which makes the story bearable for children. Four to 10 year olds would enjoy the book. It would be especially meaningful to young children who have little contact with their father.

10. Jukes, Mavis (1984). *Like Jake and Me,* New York: Alfred A. Knopf. Illustrations by Lloyd Bloom.

    This Newberry Honor Book presents a funny, interesting story of a stepfather and stepchild who have little in common. The boy is trying hard to "fit in" with Jake, who is a big brawny cowboy, and finally makes a niche when he discovers Jake is afraid of spiders and he's not. Few children have cowboys for stepfathers but they may have a stepfather very different than their biological father (in this case, an entomologist). All children will enjoy the joke of the boy describing a spider on Jake's back (Jake thinking he's describing the boys pregnant mother) and Jake taking all his clothes off trying to locate the spider. Well written book for 4-11 year olds.

11. Jukes, Mavis (1983). *No One Is Going to Nashville,* New York: Alfred A. Knopf. Illustrated by Lloyd Bloom.

   Well-written story with the stepmother playing the role of rescuer. Sonia wants to keep a stray dog that arrives at her father and stepmother's house one weekend (Sonia visits them on the weekend). A humorous and sometimes touching battle goes on between Sonia and her father over the dog. Annette who lost a favored pet as a child steps in and insists that the dog be kept, speaking up for her rights as a parent that have previously been ignored by her husband. Children 4-10 would enjoy this story about Sonia who plans to be a veterinarian and keeps a goose and a lizard at her father's house and now wants Max, the dog. Interesting stepfamily dynamics.

12. Seuling, Barbara (1985). *What Kind of Family Is This?,* Racine, WI: Western. Illustrated by Ellen Dolce.

   This is a mediocre book, certainly not compelling literature, but it brings up typical issues that occur in blended or complex stepfamily households (e.g., stepsibs having to share a room). Language used by the children is not very realistic and the "happy ending" is trite. This is probably the weakest of all the books for very young children. Four to 8 year olds might enjoy it.

13. Shyerm Marlene Fanta (1983). *Stepdog,* New York: Charles Scribner's. Illustrations by Judith Schermer.

   Funny, well-written story using a stepdog as metaphor for a stepchild. Hoover, the dog, feels left out and does naughty things to get attention (e.g., running off with people's shoes). Very upbeat story in general and an unusually happy stepfamily adjustment, but a stepchild feeling somewhat left out might develop insight from the story. Children 3-8 would enjoy it.

14. Thomas, Ianthe (1976). *Eliza's Daddy,* New York: Harcourt Brace Jovanovich. Illustrations by Moneta Barnett.

   Very nice drawings of a Black family, similar to those in the Everett Anderson books. The book is for the older preschooler or the beginning reader. Issues dealt with include child's disappointment but realization her parents would not reunite, a weekend father's indulgences, and curiosity about the father's new family (including a stepsister and half-sister). Simple, well-constructed story.

15. Vigna, Judith (1982). *Daddy's New Baby,* Niles, IL: Albert Whitman.

    A book for older preschoolers. Brings up issues very young children may or may not be able to understand ("I don't think Mommy likes Daddy's new baby. She told my Aunt we wouldn't have as much money now that Daddy has another mouth to feed."), the concept of a half-sister, jealousy of a new baby, different last names, etc. The child softens toward the baby somewhat after nearly causing her to have a serious accident.

16. Vigna, Judith (1980). *She's Not My Real Mother,* Niles, IL: Albert Whitman.

    Up to the last page it's a fairly realistic story of a boy who doesn't like his stepmother (wants his father to himself). She takes him to an ice show where he hides from her. She doesn't tell his father about the bad behavior so he tells the stepmother they can be friends. Nice story until the last page, "But Mommy doesn't have to worry-she's my only REAL mother." Issues dealt with include Mike's jealousy of Daddy's new wife, and his resentment that she interferes with their time alone together as well as the divided loyalty problem.

17. Wright, Betty Ren (1981). *My New Mom and Me,* Milwaukee: Raintree Children's Books. Illustrated by Betsy Day.

    Story of a little girl adjusting to her mother's death and beginning to adjust to her stepmother. In this, as in many other of the stepfamily books for young children, a metaphor is used for the situation. In this story, Cat, who was the mother's pet, can't adjust to the mother being gone or the presence of the stepmother. For example, when Elena feeds Cat he won't eat until she leaves. As in *Ice River* a crisis precipitates a closer relationship between the stepparent and child. In this case, Cat falls down behind the wall and is trapped when Elena and her stepdaughter are home alone. Not a truly compelling story in terms of literature, but it could be a good counseling tool for use with children 4 and up. Brings up issues typical in the grieving and adjustment process.

BOOKS FOR CHILDREN AND ADOLESCENTS

"Stepfathers in our society, however, may be duly thankful that they do not have to exchange places with some Eskimo men of whom it is written: 'The paradoxical position will occur that when a man has killed a rival in order to take his wife, he will as a loving stepfather bring up his victim's son who has some day to exact blood vengance upon him.' "

The Eskimos, (1936). Kaj Kirket-Smith. Trans. W.E. Calvert New York: E.P. Dutton, pp. 151-152. In *Stepchild,* (1953). William Carlson Smith, University of Chicago Press, p. 120.

In general, the books for adolescents are quite good. Over half the books were ranked in the two highest categories on quality. The writing style and interest level in the fiction was of universal high quality. The books are relatively brief so they can be quickly read. The content of the books does not deserve the same high praise, however. In some books, extremely negative stereotypes of stepparents are conveyed and those books seem to have little other redeeming value. Numerous books portray stereotypical situations such as a lecherous stepfather, alcoholic stepparents (alcoholism was a factor in about 10% of the books), and stepparents who physically and psychologically abuse or neglect their stepchildren. Additionally, some books dealt with divorce and remarriage as if either or both experiences immediately turned the adolescent main character into a juvenile delinquent, a poor achiever, or a depressed personality. One could only speculate about the author's purpose in writing the book. Actually, evidence from empirical research indicates that stepchildren generally function quite well (Ganong & Coleman, 1984). They are no more likely to be delinquent, to have low self-esteem, or school problems than children from intact nuclear families.

Only a few books dealt fully with the complexity of modern day stepfamilies. There were stepsibs in less than half the books for example. A handful of the books reviewed do an outstanding job of portraying stepfamily dynamics. *Me and Mr. Stenner* is exceptionally good in that situations encountered by the main character (i.e., witnessing her father become drunk and maudlin because her mother is divorcing him, being embarrassed because her mother and stepfather-to-be are living together before remarriage, innocently hurting the feelings of both her biological father and stepfather over various incidents, feeling divided loyalty) are typical of those encountered by children in divorcing families and by stepchildren. An especially appealing aspect of this book is that all adult characters (i.e., biological mother and father, stepfather) are normal, mentally healthy adults. Many stepfamily books present the stepparent as a "saint" (e.g., *The Taste of the Sweetgum Tree, Smoke*) and/or the noncustodial biological parent as extremely undesirable (e.g., *Bugs in Your Ears*).

Another problem with the books is that, although divorce is by far the most common precursor to the establishment of a stepfamily, over half the books portray death as preceding stepfamily formation. Books in which a biological parent has died are often of good literary quality but are limited in scope since they do not deal with the complexity of living in a typical, modern day stepfamily. For instance, authors can ignore the complications of having their adolescent characters relating to biological parents, stepparents, and extended family kin who may not get along with each other. Having one parent die also insures only one residence and one pair of parents for the main character. Custody issues, visitation between households, and other complexities of post-divorce stepfamilies can be ignored.

While some researchers (Bowerman & Irish, 1962) argue that children adjust to stepfamily living more readily after divorce than death, others (Duberman, 1973) disagree. The struggle of adolescents adjusting to the intrusion of a stepparent after having a parent to themselves (following the death of other parent) is poignantly told in such books as *In Our House Scott Is My Brother, Bummer Summer, Girl in the Mirror, The First Hard Times,* and *Strangers in the House.* Several of the books have haunting themes of death and suicide but are beautifully told: *A Tide Flowing, The Magic of the Glits, The Killer Swan, The Man Without a Face, Maybe It Will Rain Tomorrow.* More than 70 books (e.g., *The Empty Chair, Dark but Full of Diamonds, A Formal Feeling, Duffy, Tough Choices, Tell Me No Lies, The First Hard Times, Blowfish Live in the Sea, The UnMaking of Rabbit, Adam's Daughter, My Brother, the Thief, A Private Matter,* and the *Cloris* series) deal with one of the most common themes, the child's unresolved feelings for the absent parent. Although the adolescent characters in these books did have problems adjusting to changes in their family after death or divorce and remarriage, only in a few books (e.g., *Me & Mr. Stenner, Out of Love, Footsteps on the Stairs,* and *Things Won't Be the Same*) did main characters struggle with feelings of guilt and disloyalty (as clinicians say is typical) when they felt themselves liking and becoming attached to their stepparents. Divided loyalty was somewhat an issue in over one-third of the books, however. Working out ways to deal with two adults in the same parenting role (e.g., stepmother and biological mother) must be difficult for some stepchildren. It is also probably difficult for adolescents not in a stepfamily to even imagine. It is unfortunate there are not more books dealing with the complexity of adjusting to more than one adult in a parenting role.

A few books did present stepfamily formation via a previously unmarried mother getting married (e.g., *Harper's Mother, Tell Me No Lies, Mom, the Wolfman & Me*). The literary quality of these books was good and, with the rapidly increasing number of single females giving birth and keeping their child, the situation will probably become more common. However, in none of these books is the formation of the stepfamily central to the plot.

Another problem is that although there are approximately equal numbers of male and female stepchildren, two-thirds of the main characters in the reviewed books are female. Only a few have both males and females as main characters. This bias for female main characters may have been due to the fact that more than 80% of the authors were female; most authors featured main characters of their own sex. The preponderance of female authors may have been the reason for the disproportionately large number of stepmother families represented in the books. In reality there are at least 5 stepfather families to every 1 stepmother family. In the fiction reviewed the ratio of stepmothers to stepfathers was nearly equal.

One very positive quality of this body of literature may be that a number of books had strong main themes in addition to presenting stepfamily dynamics. For example, *A Hero Ain't Nothing But a Sandwich* dealt with drug abuse, *Tell Me No Lies* and *A Private Matter* concerned young females searching desparately for a father, and *The Empty Chair* and *A Formal Feeling* concerned girls adjusting to the death of their mothers. In *A Formal Feeling,* the main character also was adjusting to the realization that her mother had many irritating personality traits and was far from perfect. *Cloris and the Creeps, Cloris and the Freaks,* and *Cloris and the Weirdos* present a main character who is emotionally unbalanced, as does *The Scarecrows. Don't Hurt Laurie* has the theme of child abuse, in this case abuse of Laurie by her biological mother. The main character in *Girl in the Mirror* has a severe weight problem, and the main characters in *Nobody's Brother* and *The Skating Rink* stutter severely.

A few of the books reviewed dealt with impending second divorce (e.g., *In Our House Scott Is My Brother, A Father Every Few Years, One Step Apart, Cloris and the Freaks, Nobody's Brother*). Currently, about 44% of remarriages end in divorce (Glick & Spanier, 1980), a figure slightly higher than the rate of divorce for first marriages. While the situations presented in most of these books were probably typical (i.e., an immature parent in *Cloris and the Freaks, A Father Every Few Years,* and *Nobody's Brother;* stress created by incidents such as job layoffs as presented in *One Step Apart;* the hasty marriages of mismatched couples, alcohol problems, etc., as in *In Our House Scott Is My Brother*), the plot of *Cloris and the Freaks* is so depressing it would be a more appropriate book for adults. All of these books present the point of view of a child who feels victimized in the split-up of the stepfamily. In three of the books the stepsiblings had formed attachments to each other that were painful to sever and, in *Cloris and the Freaks,* one of the main characters had formed a strong attachment to her stepfather.

Another discrepancy between the books recommended and real life was that the stepfamilies in most of the books tended to be upper middle class; the setting was often California. A few notable exceptions were: *A Hero Ain't Nothin' but a Sandwich,* which was set in a Black ghetto; *Blue Willow,* a depression years story about migrant workers; *Don't Hurt Laurie,* a lower-middle to upper-class setting; *Run, Shelley, Run* and *Ollie's Go-Kart,* set in a White inner-city ghetto; and *The Skating Rink,* set in rural Georgia. The only Hispanic character in the books was the step-father, Fidel, in the *Cloris* books. He was portrayed as a warm and understanding character. Information on Jewish heritage and traditions is related in two books *(The Empty Chair* and *Happily Ever After—Almost).*

The most complex stepfamily situation of all, melding two sets of children into one family, is avoided by most authors. Only about 10% of the books presented both stepmothers and stepfathers. In the books that do feature complex stepfamilies, the high activity level and the stress within the family fairly leapt from the pages; the reader is left marveling at the resiliency of the children and adolescents who develop excellent coping skills through the course of the book. Good examples are *In Our House Scott Is My Brother, Country of Broken Stone, The Maze Stone, Cathy's Secret Kingdom, Bummer Summer, Now Is Not Too Late, Tough Choices, Things Won't Be the Same, One Step Apart, Gardine vs. Hanover, It's Just Too Much, The Animal, the Vegetable and John D. Jones,* and *Strangers in the House.*

Other characters also displayed good coping skills and made decisions reflecting maturity beyond their years: Rabbit *(UnMaking of Rabbit)* decided to stay with his grandmother who needed him, Crystal *(Tough Choices)* decided to try harder to adjust to the discipline of her father and stepmother because they were more interested in her well-being than was her mother who placed no limits upon her, and 7-year-old Lynette *(The Magic of the Glits)* found her own place to stay after her mother drowned and her new stepfather did not know what to do with her.

In addition, there are other adolescent fiction books which point out potential strengths of stepchildren. For instance, Phoebe in *The Divorce Express* states, "I feel grown up . . . like I can handle anything. I think that kids who have gone through divorces are more used to handling problems."

Only a fourth of the books were coded as featuring realistic stepfamily dynamics. This is not surprising, since the stepfamily was the main theme in less than half the books. The most common theme in the books was the child's difficulty in adjusting to change. That theme prevailed in almost half the books. Custody issues and the child's desire for the parents to reunite was a somewhat surprisingly rare theme in the books.

It is interesting to note that although only 11 empirical studies of stepfamilies had been published by 1979 (Esses & Campbell, 1979), 40-45% of the stepfamily adolescent fiction books had been published by then. Since 1979, however, the rate per year has increased greatly. The average number of stepfamily books per year from 1980-86 was 19-20. The range prior to 1980 was 0-17 (and the 17 books were published in 1979).

It appears that authors of adolescent fiction anticipated the increased interest in stepfamilies before the researchers and academicians did. Some of the more gifted authors who have also proven to be unusually and consistently insightful regarding stepfamily dynamics are C. S. Adler, Hilda Colman, Kathryn Ewing, Paula Fox, Constance Greene, Joan Lingard, Doris Buchanon Smith (though stepfamily themes are usually secondary in her books), Barbara Williams (for younger children), and Hilma Wolitzer.

References

Agnes, S. (1947). The influence of reading on the racial attitudes of adolescent girls. *The Catholic Educational Review, 45,* 415-420.

Ahrons, C., & Perlmutter, M. (1982). The relationship between former spouses: A fundamental subsystem in the remarriage family. In L. Messinger (Ed.), *Therapy with remarried families.* Rockville, MD: Aspen.

Bachrach, C. (1983). Children in families: Characteristics of biological, step-, and adopted children. *Journal of Marriage and the Family, 45,* 171-179.

Baruth, L., & Burggraf, M. (1984). The counselor and single-parent families. *Elementary School Guidance and Counseling, 19,* 30-37.

Baruth, L., & Phillips, M. (1976). Bibliotherapy and the school counselor. *School Counselor, 23,* 191-199.

Bernstein, J. (2nd ed.) (1983). *Books to help children cope with separation and loss.* New York: Bowker.

Berry, I. (1978). Contemporary bibliotherapy: Systematizing the field. In E.J. Rubin (Ed.), *Bibliotherapy Sourcebook* (pp. 185-190). Phoenix, AZ: Oryx Press.

Bitterman, C. (1968). The multimarriage family. *Social Casework, 49,* 218-221.

Bohannon, P. (1981). *Stepfamilies: A partially annotated bibliography.* Palo Alto, CA: Stepfamily Association of America.

Bowerman, C., & Irish, D. (1962). Some relationships of stepchildren and their parents. *Marriage and Family Living, 24,* 113-121.

Bowker. (1985a). *Subject guide to children's books in print 1985-1986.* New York: Bowker.

Bowker. (1985b). *Children's books in print 1985-1986.* New York: Bowker.

Bryan, H., Ganong, L., Coleman, M., & Bryan, L. (1985). Counselor's perceptions of stepparents and stepchildren. *Journal of Counseling Psychology, 32,* 279-282.

Bryan, L., Coleman, M., Ganong, L., & Bryan, H. (1986). Person perception: Family structure as a cue for stereotyping. *Journal of Marriage and the Family, 48,* 169-174.

Bryant, L., Coleman, M., & Ganong, L. (1987). *Race and family structure stereotyping.* Paper presented at the National Council on Family Relations annual conference, Atlanta, Ga.

Bulwer-Lytton (1839). *Richelieu.* Cited in B. Stevenson (Ed.) (1967), *Home book of quotations* (10th ed.). New York: Dodd, Mead.

Bumpass, L. (1984). Some characteristics of children's second families. *American Journal of Sociology, 90,* 608-623.

Cherlin, A., & McCarthy, J. (1985). Remarried couple households: Data from the June 1980 current population survey. *Journal of Marriage and the Family, 47,* 23-30.

Cherlin, A. (1978). Remarriage as an incomplete institution. *American Journal of Sociology, 84,* 634-640.

Cianciolo, P. (1965). Children's literature can affect coping behavior. *Personnel and Guidance Journal, 44,* 897-903.

Clarke-Stewart, K. (1978). Popular primers for parents. *American Psychologist, 33,* 359-369.

Coleman, M., Ganong, L., & Gingrich, R. (1985). Stepfamily strengths: A review of popular literature. *Family Relations, 34,* 583-589.

Coleman, M., Ganong, L., & Gingrich, R. (1986). Strengths of stepfamilies identified in professional literature. In S. Van Zandt (Ed.), *Building family strengths, Vol. 7* (pp. 439-451). Lincoln, NE: University of Nebraska.

Coleman, M., & Ganong, L. (1985). Remarriage myths: Implications for the helping professions. *Journal of Counseling and Development, 64,* 116-120.

Coleman, M., & Ganong, L. (1987). The cultural stereotyping of stepfamilies. In K. Pasley & M. Ihinger-Tallman (Eds.), *Remarriage and stepparenting: Current research and theory.* (pp. 19-41). New York: Guilford.

Crohn, H., Sager, C., Rodstein, E., & Walker, L. (1982). A basis for understanding and treating the remarried family. *Family Therapy Collections, 2,* 159-186.

Dreyer, S. (1977). *The bookfinder-a guide to children's literature about the needs and problems of youth aged 2-15.* Circle Pines, MN: American Guidance Service.

Dreyer, S. (1981). *The bookfinder-a guide to children's literature about the needs and problems of youth aged 2-15, Vol. 2: Annotations of books published 1975-1978.* Circle Pines, MN: American Guidance Service.

Duberman, L. (1973). Step-kin relationships. *Journal of Marriage and the Family, 35,* 283-292.

Esses, L., & Campbell, R. (1984). Challenges in researching the remarried. *Family Relations, 33,* 415-424.

Fast, I., & Cain, A. (1966). The stepparent role: Potential for disturbances in family functioning. *American Journal of Orthopsychiatry, 36,* 435-441.

Fine, M. (1986). Perceptions of stepparents: Variation in stereotypes as a function of current family structure. *Journal of Marriage and the Family, 48,* 537-543.

Fisher, F. (1968). Influence of reading and discussion on attitudes of fifth graders toward American Indians. *Journal of Educational Research, 62,* 130-134.

Fishman, B., & Hamel, B. (1981). From nuclear to stepfamily ideology: A stressful change. *Alternative Lifestyles, 4,* 181-204.

Friedman, L. (1981). Common problems in stepfamilies. In A.S. Gurman (Ed.), *Questions and answers in the practice of family therapy* (pp. 329-332). NY: Brunner/ Mazel.

Ganong, L., & Coleman, M. (1983). Stepparent: A pejorative term? *Psychological Reports, 52,* 919-922.

Ganong, L., & Coleman, M. (1984). Effects of remarriage on children: A review of the empirical literature. *Family Relations, 33,* 389-406.

Ganong, L., & Coleman, M. (1986). A comparison of clinical and empirical literature on children in stepfamilies. *Journal of Marriage and the Family, 48,* 309-318.

Ganong, L., & Coleman, M. (1987). Effects of parental remarriage on children: An updated comparison of theories, methods, and findings from clinical and empirical research. In K. Pasley & M. Ihinger-Tallman (Eds.), *Remarriage and stepparenting : Current research and theory.* (pp. 94-140). New York: Guilford.

Gardner, R. (1984). Counseling children in stepfamilies. *Elementary School Guidance and Counseling, 19,* 40-49.

Geboy, M. (1981). Who is listening to the "experts"? The use of child care materials by parents. *Family Relations, 30,* 205-210.

Gillespie, J., & Gilbert, C. (2nd) (1981). *Best books for children: Preschool through the middle grades.* New York: Bowker.

Glick, P., & Spanier, G. (1980). Married and unmarried cohabitation in the United States. *Journal of Marriage and the Family, 42,* 19-30.

Glick, P. (1984). Marriage, divorce and living arrangements: prospective changes. *Journal of Family Issues, 5,* 7-26.

Glick, P. (1987). *Demographic perspectives on remarried families.* Paper presented at the Wingspread Conference on Remarried Families, Racine, WI.

Goldner, V. (1982). Remarriage family: Structure, system, future. In J.C. Hansen & L. Messinger (Eds.), *Therapy with remarried families* (pp. 187-206). Rockville, MD: Aspen.

Gottschalk, L. (1948). Bibliotherapy as an adjuvant in psychotherapy. *American Journal of Psychiatry, 104,* 632-637.

Greif, G. (1982). The father-child relationship subsequent to divorce. In J. Hansen & L. Messinger (Eds.), *Therapy with remarried families* (pp. 47-57). Rockville, MD: Aspen.

Griffin, B. (1984). *Special needs bibliography: Current books for/about children and young adults.* DeWitt, NY: Griffin.

Heminghaus, E. (1954). *The effect of bibliotherapy on the attitudes and personal and social adjustment of a group of elementary school children.* Unpublished doctoral dissertation, Washington University. Dissertation Abstracts International 14, 1641.

Hughes, R., & Durio, H. (1983). Patterns of childcare information seeking by families. *Family Relations, 32,* 203-212.

Hynes, A., & Hynes-Berry, M. (1986). *Bibliotherapy-The interactive process: A handbook.* Boulder, CO: Westview.

Isaacs, M. (1982). Facilitating family restructuring and relinkage. In J. Hansen & L. Messinger (Eds.), *Therapy With Remarried Families* (pp. 121-143). Rockville, MD: Aspen.

Jacobson, D. (1979). Stepfamilies: Myths and realities. *Social Work, 24,* 202-207.

Jacobson, D. (1984, April). *Family type, visiting, and children's behavior in the stepfamily: A linked family system.* Paper presented at the annual meeting of the American Orthopsychiatric Association, Toronto, Ontario.

Jalongo, M. (1983). Using crisis-oriented books with young children. *Young Children, 39,* 29-36.

Jones, S. (1978). Remarriage: A new beginning, a new set of problems. *Journal of Divorce, 2,* 217-227.

Kompara, D. (1980). Difficulties in the socialization of stepparenting. *Family Relations, 29,* 69-73.

Lutz, P. (1983). The stepfamily: An adolescent perspective. *Family Relations, 32,* 367-376.

McGoldrick, M., & Carter, E. (1980). Forming a remarried family. In E. Carter & M. McGoldrick (Eds.), *The family life cycle* (pp. 265-294). NY: Gardner Press.

McInnes, K. (1982). Bibliotherapy: Adjunct to traditional counseling with children of stepfamilies. *Child Welfare, 61,* 153-160.

McKinney, F. (1977). Exploration in bibliotherapy. *Personnel and Guidance Journal, 56,* 550-552.

Messinger, L. (1984). *Remarriage: A family affair.* New York: Plenum.

Messinger, L., & Walker, K. (1981). From marriage breakdown to remarriage: Parental tasks and therapeutic guidelines. *American Journal of Orthopsychiatry, 51,* 429-438.

Miller, M., & Saper, B. (1982). An emerging contingency, the stepfamily: Review of literature. *Psychological Reports, 50,* 715-722.

Mills, D. (1984). A model for stepfamily development. *Family Relations, 33,* 365-372.

Mowatt, M. (1972). Group psychotherapy for stepfathers and their wives. *Psychotherapy: Theory, Research, and Practice, 9,* 328-331.

National Council on Family Relations Focus Group on Remarriage and Stepfamilies (1987). *Remarriage and Stepparenting: A comprehensive bibliography.* Unpublished bibliography.

Nolan, J., Coleman, M., & Ganong, L. (1984). The presentation of stepfamilies in marriage and family textbooks. *Family Relations, 33,* 559-566.

Papernow, P. (1984). The stepfamily cycle: An experimental model of stepfamily development. *Family Relations, 33,* 355-364.

Piaget, J. (1973). *Language and thoughts of the child.* New York: World.

Podolsky, E. (1955). The emotional problems of the stepchild. *Mental Hygiene, 39,* 49-53.

Rubin, R. (1978). *Using bibliotherapy: A guide to theory and practice.* Phoenix, AZ: Oryx Press.

Russell, D., & Shrodes, C. (1950). Contributions of research in bibliotherapy of the language arts program. *School Review, 58,* 338-342.

Sager, C., Brown, H., Crohn, H., Engel, T., & Rodstein, E. (1983). *Treating the remarried family.* NY: Brunner/Mazel.

Schrank, F., & Engels, D. (1981). Bibliotherapy as a counseling adjunct: Research findings. *Personnel and Guidance Journal, 60,* 143-147.

Schultheis, M. (1972). *A guidebook for bibliotherapy.* Glenview, IL: Psychotechnics.

Stanton, G. (1986). Preventive intervention with stepfamilies. *Social Work, 31,* 201-206.

Visher, E., & Visher, J. (1979). *Stepfamilies: A guide to working with stepparents and stepchildren.* NY: Brunner/Mazel.

Visher, E., & Visher, J. (1982). Stepfamilies in the 1980s. In J. C. Hansen & L. Messenger (Eds.), *Therapy with remarried families* (pp. 105-119). Rockville, MD: Aspen.

Wald, E. (1981). *The remarried family: Challenge and promise.* NY: Family Service Association of America.

Walker, K., & Messinger, L. (1979). Remarriage after divorce: Dissolution and reconstruction of family boundaries. *Family Process, 18,* 185-192.

Webster's New Collegiate Dictionary. (1981). Springfield, MA: Merriam-Webster.

Whiteside, M. (1981). A family systems approach with families of remarriage. In I. Stuart & L. Abt (Eds.), *Children of separation and divorce* (pp. 319-337). NY: Van Nostrand Reinhold.

Whiteside, M. (1982). Remarriage: A family developmental approach. *Journal of Marital and Family Therapy, 4,* 59-68.

Whiteside, M. (1983). Families of remarriage: The weaving of many life cycle threads. *Family Therapy Collections, 7,* 100-119.

Winkel, L. (13th) (1982). *The elementary school library collection: A guide to books and other media.* Newark, NJ: The Bro-Dart Foundation.

Winkel, L. (15th) (1986). *The elementary school library collection: A guide to books and other media.* Newark, NJ: The Bro-Dart Foundation.

Zaccaria, J. & Moses, H. (1968). *Facilitating human development through reading: The use of bibliotherapy in teaching and counseling.* Champaign, IL: Stipes.

CHAPTER 4

REVIEWING STEPFAMILY SELF-HELP BOOKS FOR CHILDREN AND ADOLESCENTS

Locating the Self-Help Books

SOME OF THE self-help books were located while searching for fiction. The majority of the references, however, were obtained via computer searches of major reference banks, published bibliographies (Bohannon, 1981; NCFR Focus Group on Remarriage and Stepfamilies, 1987), referrals from colleagues, and standard library search methods.

A total of 12 self-help books were located. Two were written for adolescents, 8 were written for children, and 2 were appropriate for both young adolescents and older children.

Reviewing the Self-Help Books

A coding scheme was developed prior to reviewing the books. The code was designed to identify: a) stepfamily issues and concerns, b) stepfamily strengths, and c) advice. The initial coding scheme was based on earlier reviews of the research and clinical literature on stepchildren and their families (Ganong & Coleman, 1984; 1986; 1987). New coding categories were added as they were encountered in the self-help books.

Each reference was initially examined thoroughly and coded by one of us and all were read by both of us. A reading specialist served as a consultant. Self-help materials were coded for the following:

1. Appropriate audience (adolescents or school age children)
2. Background of author (journalist, educator, counselor, stepparent, stepchild)
3. Stepfamily issues identified

49

4. Advice given
5. Stepfamily strengths presented
6. Type of references cited (i.e., clinical, popular, or empirical bases of information, number of references)
7. General interest and quality of writing style (1-10 scale)
8. Recommended/not recommended (based on quality of writing, soundness of information/advice presented, range of stepfamily issues covered)

Appropriate Audience

The two books written specifically for adolescents were by Craven (1982) and Getzoff and McClenahan (1984). Three other books for children (as indicated by the authors) are also appropriate for adolescents, at least young adolescents (Gardner, 1982; Hyde, 1981; LeShan, 1978). In fact, in our opinion, the Gardner book is more appropriate for adolescents than children, due to the reading level and the comprehensiveness of the material. In addition, two books were designed for parents and children to read together (Burt & Burt, 1983, Lewis, 1980), and four books have either an introduction or afterword for parents (Gardner, 1982; Lewis, 1980; Phillips, 1981; Stenson, 1979). Two other books have sections that are for parents, or appear to be for parents, in the body. Bradley (1982) has a section called "Resources for Parents" and Getzoff and McClenahan (1984) have a section on how to hold a family council. Actually, all of the books could probably be read and appreciated by parents.

Background of Author

It is perhaps not surprising, but important to note, that 5 of the books (Burt & Burt, 1983; Craven, 1982; Getzoff & McClenahan, 1984; Lewis, 1980; Stenson, 1979) were written by clinicians who are themselves stepparents. Bradley (1982) is a journalist as well as a stepparent, and Phillips (1981) indicated she was a stepchild. LeShan (1978) and Gardner (1982) did not identify themselves as stepparents, only clinicians, and Hyde (1981) and Berman (1982) are journalists who did not identify themselves as stepparents. It may be that those who live or have lived in stepfamilies have a special appreciation for the nuances of living in a stepfamily situation and want to share their personal as well as professional insight.

Stepfamily Issues Identified

Nearly 50 different issues or problems were mentioned in these self-help books. Two issues, what to call the stepparent, or "names," and problems related to merging different family styles, were mentioned most often (12 books), followed by loyalty conflicts (10), stepsibling conflicts (10), discipline (9), myth of the wicked stepparent (9), the myth of instant love (8), and jealousy (7). Most of these issues address the transition period following parental remarriage. For example, what to call the stepparent, merging two families, space issues, discipline, and the myth of instant love between stepparent and child are concerns related to a child's adjustment to a parental remarriage. This focus seems reasonable, since clinicians have identified that the experience of adjusting to a parental remarriage is the most stressful and problematic time for children (Visher & Visher, 1979), and a time when self-help books might most likely be read (Cianciolo, 1965; McInnis, 1982).

The issues presented in these books are congruent with those issues identified by clinical writers as problem areas for stepfamilies (Ganong & Coleman, 1986, 1987). This is not particularly surprising, since a majority of the authors are clinicians themselves. This congruence is potentially helpful to lay readers who may obtain one of these self-help books on their own in a search for answers to their problems.

Advice Given

For ease and clarity of presentation, the advice given has been divided into three areas: communication, things to consider, and things to do.

Communication. Many suggestions regarding communication were quite specific and concrete. For example, children were advised to tell their stepparent what they want to call them (Craven, 1982; Gardner, 1982; Lewis, 1980), to say "thank you" when people do nice things for them (Gardner, 1982), and to tell their stepmother what foods they like (Getzoff & McClenahan, 1984). Some authors gave direct advice on communication without accompanying concrete examples of what to actually say. For example, children were advised to try out different names for the stepparent until they found one that "fit" (Lewis, 1980), to try out different ways to introduce the stepparent (Lewis, 1980), and to talk directly to the stepparent rather than using the parent as an intermediary (Lewis, 1980). They were also advised to tell "lovey-dovey" adults if such behavior is embarrassing to them (Craven, 1982), to express anger in a polite way and before it grows (Gardner, 1982), to ask questions (Gardner, 1982; LeShan,

1978), and to tell others when they are making the stepchild feel uncomfortable (Craven, 1982; Lewis, 1982). Stepchildren were cautioned to express feelings about things in a nonthreatening and nonangry way (Craven, 1982; Getzoff & McClenahan, 1984). They were counseled to ask stepparents things they want to know about them (Lewis, 1980), to make their expectations clear (Craven, 1982), to share feelings (Nickman, 1986), to inform new family members of sore spots to avoid (Craven, 1982), and to sit down with stepsiblings and set up rules about sharing (Craven, 1982). Additional advice offered included discussing the new stepparent's role in discipline (Craven, 1982), asking for what you want and need when visiting the other household or when stepsiblings visit (Craven, 1982), and telling someone when physical abuse is happening (Craven, 1982). Bradley (1982) provided specific examples of ways to word questions, such as "Do I have to love her?" "Do I have to do as he says?" and statements such as "I want you to spend more time with me; I'm lonely." Such examples are helpful to children and adolescents who may have difficulty comprehending admonitions to "communicate feelings" to stepparents and parents.

Advice related to communication also was addressed to adult readers in prefaces, introductions, or afterwords. These directives centered on making expectations clear (Phillips, 1981), discussing adult's concerns with the children (Stenson, 1979), and telling the children that the stepparent will have a say in how they will be raised (Stenson, 1979). Biological parents were advised to let children know they will still be loved and cared for (Bradley, 1982).

Things to Consider. Some of the advice coded as things to consider was related to communication in the stepfamily. For example, stepchildren were advised that family meetings are a good way to reduce or resolve problems (Gardner, 1982; Hyde, 1981) and that they should not be pressured into feeling obligated to call a stepparent "mom" or "dad" (Craven, 1982; Getzoff & McLenahan, 1984; Lewis, 1980; Stenson, 1979). Stepchildren also were advised that stepparents sometimes make mistakes because they lack information and they should not hesitate to supply that information to stepmoms and stepdads (Getzoff & McClanahan, 1984; Lewis, 1980).

Most of the things to consider were ideas for stepchild readers to think about. Some of these gave permission for stepchildren to accept their feelings; variations of the notion that love takes time to grow and love may never develop between stepparents and children — were mentioned frequently (e.g., Craven, 1982; Getzoff & McClanahan, 1984).

Advice regarding the uniqueness of stepfamilies, e.g., "remember that being different is neither good nor bad" was given (Gardner, 1982) as were suggestions addressing the problem of loyalty conflicts (Bradley, 1982; Stenson, 1979). Bromides about control, such as "remarriage isn't your decision" (Gardner, 1982) and "recognize what you can control versus what you can't" (Gardner, 1982) were given. Also addressed were myths of wicked stepparents (Gardner, 1982), advice on liking or not liking stepsiblings (Bradley, 1982), and ways to adapt to two different households, presented as "when in Rome, do as the Romans do" (Gardner, 1982).

Things to Do. This category included some vaguely-stated advice, such as "don't force yourself to be cheerful and busy all the time" (LeShan, 1978), as well as quite explicit advice such as "don't slither in and out of the house without speaking to your stepparent" (Getzhoff & McClenahan, 1984) and "pick up after yourself" (Getzhoff & McClenahan, 1984). The most clear, concrete advice regarding things to do were found in books by Craven (1982), Getzhoff and McClenahan (1984), Gardner (1982), and Bradley (1982).

Strengths Presented

Identified strengths associated with living in a stepfamily were few in number. Not surprisingly, more issues/problems were identified than strengths or advantages of parental remarriage. The books ranged from Hyde (1981) who mentioned no strengths to Getzhoff and McClenahan (1984) who mentioned 13. The average number of strengths mentioned was 4.5. The availability of more adults for providing new experiences (8 books) and more presents and cards at birthdays and holidays (5 books) were often mentioned. Having a stepparent is cited as an advantage in a variety of ways. A happy remarriage presents to children a positive model of adult intimacy and marriage (2 books). The stepparent and child may enter into a real positive, special relationship with each other (4 books). Stepparents also may add stability to a child's home (2 books) and the biological parent may be happier as a result of the remarriage, making life more pleasant for the child (5 books). Children also are encouraged to consider long-term advantages. Stepchildren potentially become more adaptable people, able to flexibly deal with life as adults (2 books).

References Cited

None of the books contained references of either empirical or clinical research in the body or in a reference list. Nor were any other self-help books referred to by these authors in the text. However, 3 books listed self-help books for children in a reference list (Bradley, 1982; Burt & Burt, 1983; Getzoff & McClenahan, 1984), 3 listed self-help books for adults (Bradley, 1982; Getzoff & McClenahan, 1984; Hyde, 1981), and 3 had fiction for children listed (Bradley, 1982; Burt & Burt, 1983; Getzoff & McClenahan, 1984; Hyde, 1981; LeShan, 1978).

General Interest/Writing Style

The judgment of writing style was subjective but there was high agreement between the authors and the reading consultant on this variable. In general, the books were considered to be well-written and easily held the reader's attention. Two criteria were used to evaluate the quality of the writing: how interesting the book was to read, and how appropriate the level of reading difficulty was for the target age for whom the book was designed. The books generally were interesting to read and appropriate for the audience. Phillips's (1981) tone was somewhat stilted; it seemed to be written **to** children instead of **for** children. The workbook written by Burt and Burt (1983) demanded a level of cognitive and verbal sophistication that often seemed too advanced for the example problems described in the workbook. A child capable and willing to do these activities with parents may find some of the activities seem designed for younger children.

Recommendations

Several criteria were used in determining whether or not to recommend books for adolescents, children, parents, and stepparents. First, the number of issues and problems discussed were taken into account. Generally, the more issues dealt with, the better the overall quality of the book. Second, the quantity and quality of advice given was considered. Clear, concrete advice is most effective with children. If advice is to be useful it must be within the abilities of most children. Third, the number of strengths discussed were considered. Fourth, the reading difficulty and quality of writing were considered. Although these are slippery concepts, our evaluations were based on years of training in child development and education and a reading specialist was consulted to validate our judgements. Fifth, "extras" such as illustrations and prefaces for parents and stepparents were considered. Such extras enhance the appeal of books to both children and adults. In general, books were rated more highly if they could be useful to both children and adults in stepfamilies.

Based on these criteria, the most highly recommended books were those by Bradley (1982), Craven (1982), and Lewis (1980). Books written by Berman (1982), Getzoff and McClenahan (1984), Hyde (1981), LeShan (1978), and Stenson (1979) were recommended, but not as heartily. Three books were recommended with reservations (Burt & Burt, 1983; Phillips, 1981). All of the books were perceived to be of some value. A brief description of each of these self-help references follows.

SELF-HELP BOOKS
FOR CHILDREN AND ADOLESCENTS

1. Craven, L. (1982). Stepfamilies: New Patterns of Harmony. New York: Messner.

    Craven's was the most highly recommended book for adolescents. It contained a comprehensive overview of special problems and issues adolescents in stepfamilies might face. Perhaps more importantly, it contained a high number of potential strengths to be found in stepfamilies and the advice given covered most of the problems identified in the clinical literature. It is well-written but does contain some unsupported assertions (e.g., "the average adjustment time for stepfamilies is about 5 years," p. 24).

2. Getzoff, A., & McClenahan, C. (1984). Stepkids: A Survival Guide for Teenagers in Stepfamilies and for Stepparents Doubtful of Their Own Survival. New York: Walker.

    This contains a great deal of good information, much of which would be good for parents to read. There are five appendices which offer useful information for both adolescents and parents. The book is designed for adolescents and has an especially good section (with specific examples) on communicating within the stepfamily. One amusing but excellent practical section deals with special gripes stepmothers have (e.g., "Don't eat 'special' food — if you have any doubt about what to eat, ask.") and special gripes stepfathers have (e.g., "Don't waste food, water, gas, or anything."). This book, as does Bradley's (1982), has a good section on why the absent parent may not visit. A drawback of this book is that it sometimes seemed repetitive and would, therefore, have less appeal for teenagers.

3. Hyde, M. (1981). My Friend Has Four Parents. New York: McGraw-Hill.

    This book was written for younger adolescents and school age children. Only 1 of 6 chapters was on stepfamilies. The book also covers divorce, single-parent custody, and parental kidnapping.

4. LeShan, E. (1978). What's going to happen to me? When parents separate or divorce. New York: Four Winds Press.

In LeShan's book, 3 of the 5 chapters were about divorce and only one chapter was about stepfamilies. This is another book that is appropriate for younger adolescents as well as children.

5. Nickman, S. (1986). Help! My parents are driving me crazy. New York: Messner.

This book, written for older children or younger adolescents, was perhaps the most limited in scope of any of the self-help books. Only one brief chapter is on stepfamilies and half of it is a story of a boy going to meet his dad's new family. Consequently, few issues are discussed and only one strength is mentioned. The advice is broad (e.g., work out problems with stepsiblings).

6. Gardner, R. (1982). The boys' and girls' book about stepfamilies. New York: Bantam.

Gardner states his book is for children, but it would take an extremely intelligent and highly motivated child to tackle this extremely comprehensive book. The chapters are quite long and there is a great deal of printed material on each page. It would appear much more appropriate for adolescents. The book is illustrated and contains an introduction for adults as well as children. Many examples are given throughout the book.

7. Bradley, B. (1982). Where do I belong? A kids guide to stepfamilies. Reading, MA: Addison-Wesley.

The Bradley book is written for children (grade school age) and contains a good section on divorce and issues for children surrounding divorce. This book has an attractive layout and cute pictures that show children of different racial and ethnic characteristics. It also contains a very helpful explanation of why noncustodial parents often do not visit their children.

8. Lewis, H. C. (1980). All about families the second time around. Atlanta: Peachtree.

Lewis is also written for children, and though few strengths are specifically identified, overall the book is positive with a heavy emphasis on normal feelings. Pictures with various races are displayed throughout the book. A preface for both adults and children is included along with activities for children to do. This book is recommended, but the reading level seems difficult for the age targeted (early primary grades).

9. Stenson, J. (1979). Now I have a stepparent and it's kind of confusing. New York: Avon.

The Stenson book was designed for parents or stepparents to read to or with their children. The two page preface for adults is well written and full of information and advice. This illustrated book is a story told in the first person by a child whose parents divorce, then his mother begins to date and eventually remarries. The book is visually appealing, with black-and-white line drawings on every page.

10. Burt, M. & Burt, B. (1983). What's special about our stepfamily? New York: Doubleday.

   This book also is a workbook designed for children to work on with their parents. It is likely, however, that children old enough to complete the activities would be uncomfortable filling it out with their parents as the information is very personal. There is a parent section in the back of the book that contains stepfamily issues and a preface for adults as well as a preface for children.

11. Phillips, C. (1981). Our family got a stepparent. Ventura, CA: Regal.

   This is the only book reviewed with any specific religious overtones, although religion is not an overriding theme. It is a story book with pictures, but it is less visually appealing than the other books. An advice to stepparents/"natural" parents section is included in the appendix.

12. Berman, C. (1982). What am I doing in a stepfamily? Secaucus, NJ: Lyle Stuart.

   Berman contains very attractive colored pictures on each page but the content and appearance of the book are incongruent. The size and pictures suggest that it is a preschool book, but the text is definitely for older children. This book even contains some demographic data about stepfamilies — information that seems quite inappropriate in a book for young children. Advice given in this book is often too abstract or expects too much of young children (e.g., "It's a good idea to tell your stepparent how you feel about things."). Though two strengths were mentioned they were pretty feeble attempts (i.e., "getting to know and like so many people [and having them like you] is one of the best parts of what being in a stepfamily — **your** stepfamily — is all about," and you get lots of cards on your birthday).

   It should be noted again that the self-help books reviewed here are not for the stepchild having severe emotional problems. The books are designed to educate the child about stepfamily living and to provide insight to the child having mild to moderate problems in adjusting to stepfamily living. They also, in some cases, provide information that may help a child avoid problems in the future.

References

Bohannan, P. (1981). *Stepfamilies: A partially annotated bibliography.* Palo Alto, CA: Stepfamily Association of American, Inc.

Cianciolo, P. (1965). Children's literature can affect coping behavior. *Personnel and Guidance Journal, 44,* 897-903.

Ganong, L., & Coleman, M. (1984). Effects of remarriage on children: A review of the empirical literature. *Family Relations, 33,* 389-406.

Ganong, L., & Coleman, M. (1986). A comparison of clinical and empirical literature on children in stepfamilies. *Journal of Marriage and the Family, 48,* 309-318.

Ganong, L., & Coleman, M. (1987). Effects of stepfamilies on children: An updated comparison of theories, methods, and findings from clinical and empirical research. In K. Pasley & M. Inhinger-Tallman (Eds.), *Remarriage and stepparenting: Current research and theory* (pp. 94-140). New York: Guilford.

McInnes, K. (1982). Bibliotherapy: Adjunct to traditional counseling with children of stepfamilies. *Child Welfare, 61,* 153-160.

National Council on Family Relations Focus Group on Remarriage and Stepparenting. (1987). *Bibliography on remarriage and stepparenting.* Author.

Visher, E., & Visher, J. (1979). *Stepfamilies: A guide to working with stepparents and stepchildren.* New York: Brunner/Mazel.

CLASSIFICATION GUIDE

CLASSIFICATION GUIDE

	Title	Author	Publisher	Age of [a]MC	Sex of [b]MC	Literary Quality [c]Rating	Stepfamily Theme
1.	Footsteps on the Stairs (1982)	Adler, C.S.	Delacorte	13	F	5	Central
2.	In Our House Scott is My Brother (1980)	Adler, C.S.	Macmillan	13	F	5	Central
3.	The Magic of the Glits (1979)	Adler, C.S.	Macmillan	12	M	5	Central
4.	Binding Ties (1985)	Adler, C.S.	Delacorte	16	F	3	Incidental
5.	Fly Free (1984)	Adler, C.S.	Coward-McCann	13	F	5	Secondary
6.	Split Sisters (1986)	Adler, C.S.	Macmillan	11	F	5	Central
7.	Lisa's Choice (1979)	Aks, Patricia	Ballantine Books	15	F	5	Central
8.	Duffy (1972)	Alcock, Gudrun	Wm. Morrow	11	F	4	Central
9.	Conjuring Summer In (1986)	Ames, Mildred	Harper & Row Junior Books	16	F	4	Secondary
10.	Springtime for Eva (1959)	Anckarsvard, Karin	Harcourt, Brace, Jovanovich	16	F	3	Incidental
11.	The Whistling Boy (1969)	Arthur, Ruth M.	Atheneum	16	F	4 or 5	Central
12.	Missing Pieces (1984)	Asher, Sandy	Delacorte	16	F/M	4	Secondary
13.	Break in the Sun (1980)	Ashley, Bernard	S.G. Phillips	11	F	2-3	Central
14.	A Father Every Few Years (1977)	Bach, Alice	Harper & Row	11	M	4	Central
15.	Bugs in Your Ears (1977)	Bates, Betty	Holiday House	13	F	3	Central
16.	Thatcher Payne-in-the-Neck (1985)	Bates, Betty	Holiday House	10	F	3	Secondary
17.	Shelter From the Wind (1976)	Bauer, Marion Dane	Clarion	12	F	4	Central
18.	The Robbers (1979)	Bawden, Nina	Lothrop Lee & Shepard	9	M	4	Incidental

Title	Author	Publisher	Age of [a]MC	Sex of [b]MC	Literary Quality [c]Rating	Stepfamily Theme
19. Rebel on a Rock (1978)	Bawden, Nina	Lippincott	12	F	5	Incidental
20. The Coach that Never Came (1985)	Beatty, Patricia	Wm. Morrow	13	M	2	Incidental
21. The Wicked Stepdog (1982)	Benjamin, Carol L.	Crowell	11	F	3	Central
22. Nuisance (1983)	Berger, Fredericka	Wm. Morrow	13	F	3	Central
23. Stepchild (1980)	Berger, Terry	Messner	12	M	4	Central
24. Puppy Love (1986)	Betancourt, Jeanne	Avon Books	13	F	4	Central
25. A Gathering of Days: A New England Girl's Journal 1830-32 (1979)	Blos, Joan	Scribners	14	F	5	Secondary
26. Country of Broken Stone (1980)	Bond, Nancy	Atheneum	14	F	5	Secondary
27. Gimme an H, Gimme an E, Gimme an L, Gimme a P (1980)	Bonham, Frank	Scribners	16	M/F	3	Secondary
28. In Her Father's Footsteps (1976)	Bradbury, Bianca	Houghton Mifflin	17	F	2	Central
29. Where's Jim Now? (1978)	Bradbury, Bianca	Houghton Mifflin	14	M	2	Central
30. Those Traver Kids (1972)	Bradbury, Bianca	Houghton Mifflin	17	F	2	Central
31. A Year in the Life of Rosie Bernard (1971)	Brenner, Barbara	Harper & Row	10	F	4	Central
32. Kate Crackernuts (1979)	Briggs, K.M.	Greenwillow	6-15	F	2	Central
33. The Swing of the Gate (1978)	Brown, Roy	Clarion	20	M	4	Incidental
34. The Animal, The Vegetable, and John D. Jones (1982)	Byars, Betsy	Delacorte	Preadol.	2 F; 1 M	4	Central
35. The Half Sisters (1970)	Carlson, Natalie	Harper & Row	12	F	2	Central
36. To Touch the Deer (1981)	Cazzola, Gus	Westminster	Adol.	M	5	Secondary
37. A Hero Ain't Nothin' But a Sandwich (1973)	Childress, Alice	Coward, McCann & Geoghegan	13	M	5	Central
38. Early Rising (1974)	Clarke, Joan	Lippincott	6-16	F	2-3	Secondary
39. Moon Lake Angel (1987)	Cleaver, Vera	Lothrop, Lee & Shepard	10	F	2-3	Incidental

Title	Author	Publisher	Age of ªMC	Sex of ᵇMC	Literary Quality ᶜRating	Stepfamily Theme
40. The Killer Swan (1980)	Clifford, Eth	Houghton Mifflin	Adol.	M	4	Secondary
41. Don't Fence Me In (1984)	Cole, Brenda	Siloutte	16	F	3	Secondary
42. Tell Me No Lies (1978)	Colman, Hila	Crown	12	F	4	Secondary
43. Just the Two of Us (1984)	Colman, Hila	Scholastic Inc.	15	F	5	Secondary
44. Weekend Sisters (1985)	Colman, Hila	Wm. Morrow	14	F	5	Secondary
45. What I Did for Roman (1987)	Conrad, Paul	Harper & Row	15	F	4	Sec./Inc.
46. Lanky Jones (1980)	Cookson, Catherine	Macdonald Futura	15	M	3	Incidental
47. Isle of the Shape-Shifters (1983)	Coonty, Otto	Houghton Mifflin	12	F	3	Incidental
48. Smoke (1967)	Corbin, William	Coward, McCann & Geoghegan	14 +	M	4	Central
49. The Person in the Potting Shed (1980)	Corcoran, Barbara	Atheneum	Adol.	F	2-3	Secondary
50. Stranger on the Road (1971)	Crane, Caroline	Random House	15	F	4	Central
51. In the Long Run (1987)	Crisp, N. J.	Viking	14	F	4	Incidental
52. Chartbreaker (1986)	Cross, Gillian	Holiday House	17	F	3	Secondary
53. Billy Beg and the Bull (1978)	Curley, Daniel	Crowell	?	M	2	Central
54. The Divorce Express (1982)	Danziger, Paula	Delacorte	14	F	4-5	Incidental
55. Stepsister Sally (1952)	Daringer, Helen F.	Harcourt, Brace, Jovanovich	11	F	3	Central
56. Dear Stepmother (1956)	De Leeuw, Adele and Paradis, Marjorie	Macmillan	17	F	3	Secondary
57. Angel's Mother's Boyfriend (1986)	Delton, Judy	Houghton Mifflin	10	F	4	Secondary
58. And Philippa Makes Four (1983)	Derman, Martha	Four Winds Press	12	F	3	Central
59. Healer (1983)	Dickinson, Peter	Delacorte	16, 10	M, F	2	Incidental
60. I'll Get There. It Better Be Worth the Trip (1969)	Donovan, John	Harper Row	11-13	M	2	Secondary
61. My Mother's Getting Married (1986)	Drescher, Joan	Dial Books	6 or 7	F	4	Central
62. Locked in Time (1985)	Duncan, Lois	Little, Brown	17	F	3	Central

Title	Author	Publisher	Age of [a]MC	Sex of [b]MC	Literary Quality [c]Rating	Stepfamily Theme
63. The Twisted Window (1987)	Duncan, Lois	Delacorte	17	F	4	Secondary
64. The Maze Stone (1982)	Dunlop, Eileen	Coward-McCann	15	F	5	Incidental
65. Stepfamily (1980)	Emery, Anne	Westminster	14	F	4-5	Central
66. Under the Haystack (1973)	Engebrecht, P.A.	Thomas Nelson	13	F	2	Incidental
67. A Private Matter (1975)	Ewing, Kathryn	Harcourt, Brace, Jovanovich	9	F	5	Incidental
68. Things Won't Be the Same (1980)	Ewing, Kathryn	Harcourt, Brace, Jovanovich	10	F	5	Central
69. The Phaedra Complex (1971)	Eyerly, Jeanette	Lippincott	16	F	2	Central
70. See Dave Run (1978)	Eyerly, Jeanette	Pocket Books	15	M	3	Central
71. Drop-Out (1963)	Eyerly, Jeanette	Lippincott	16	F	3	Incidental
72. The World of Ellen March (1964)	Eyerly, Jeanette	Lippincott	16	F	3	Incidental
73. Cathy's Secret Kingdom (1963)	Faber, Nancy	Lippincott	11	F	4	Incidental
74. Who Is Erika? (1959)	Falk, Ann Marie	Harcourt, Brace, & World	15	F	4	Central
75. The Glass Slipper (1984)	Farjeon, Eleanor	Lippincott	16	F	3	Central
76. Ms. Isabelle Cornell, Herself (1980)	Farley, Carol	Atheneum	12	F	4	Secondary
77. Sophia Scarlotta and Ceecee (1979)	Feagles, Anita McRae	Atheneum	16	F	4	Incidental
78. Rachel Vellers, How Could You (1984)	Fisher, Lois I.	Dodd, Mead	11	F	4	Incidental
79. Sport (1979)	Fitzhugh, Louise	Delacorte	11	M	4	Secondary
80. The Pumpkin Shell (1981)	Forman, James	Farrar, Straus & Giroux	18	M	3	Central
81. Mrs. Abercorn and the Bunce Boys (1986)	Fosburgh, Liza	Macmillian (Four Winds Press)	12	M	4	Secondary
82. Blowfish Live in the Sea (1970)	Fox, Paula	Bradbury	13	M & F	5	Secondary

Title	Author	Publisher	Age of ^aMC	Sex of ^bMC	Literary Quality ^cRating	Stepfamily Theme
83. A Place Apart (1980)	Fox, Paula	Farrar, Straus, Giroux	13	F	5	Incidental
84. The Flint Hills Foal (1976)	Francis, Dorothy B.	Abingdon	10	F	4	Secondary
85. Reasons To Stay (1986)	Froehlich, Margaret Walden	Houghton Mifflin	12	F	4	Incidental
86. Blue Willow (1940)	Gates, Doris	Viking	10	F	5	Incidental
87. Please Don't Kiss Me Now (1981)	Gerber, Merrill Joan	Dial	15	F	2	Secondary
88. How I Put My Mother Through College (1981)	Gerson, Corinne	Atheneum	13	F	2	Incidental
89. Danny (1979)	Gessner, Lynne	Harvey House	16	M	3	Incidental
90. Ask Me If I Care (1985)	Gilmour, H.B.	Ballantine Books	14	F	5	Incidental
91. Branigan's Dog (1981)	Grace, Fran	Bradbury Press	15	M	5	Central
92. Joshua Fortune (1980)	Grant, Cynthia	Atheneum	14	M	2	Central
93. Jane Hope (1933)	Gray, Elizabeth	Viking	12-16	F	3	Secondary
94. The UnMaking of Rabbit (1972)	Greene, Constance	Viking	11	M	5	Incidental
95. I Know You, Al (1975)	Greene, Constance	Dell Yearling	12 or 13	F	4	Central
96. Getting Nowhere (1977)	Greene, Constance	Viking	14	M	5	Central
97. I and Sproggy (1978)	Greene, Constance	Viking	10	M	3	Central
98. Your Old Pal, Al (1979)	Greene, Constance	Viking	12 or 13	F	5	Central
99. Al(exandra) the Great (1982)	Greene, Constance	Viking	12 or 13	F	5	Central
100. There's a Caterpillar in My Lemonade (1980)	Gregory, Diana	Addison-Wesley	14	F	3	Secondary
101. The Dog at the Window (1984)	Griffiths, Helen	Holiday House	12	F	4	Secondary
102. Wait Till Helen Comes (1986)	Hahn, Mary Downing	Clarion Books	12	F	3	Secondary
103. Uphill All the Way (1984)	Hall, Lynn	Schribner's Sons	17	F	5	Incidental
104. The Swing (1979)	Hanlon, Emily	Bradbury	11, 11	M, F	4	Central

Title	Author	Publisher	Age of [a]MC	Sex of [b]MC	Literary Quality [c]Rating	Stepfamily Theme
105. Watcher in the Dark (1986)	Hastings, Beverly	Berkley	17	F	4	Incidental
106. Two Under Par (1987)	Henkes, Kevin	Greenwillow	10	M	4	Central
107. The Man Without a Face (1972)	Holland, Isabelle	Lippincott	14	M	4	Secondary
108. Now Is Not Too Late (1980)	Holland, Isabelle	Lothrop	11	F	4	Secondary
109. Of Love and Death and Other Journeys (1975)	Holland, Isabelle	Lippincott	15	F	5	Secondary
110. Mama & Her Boys (1981)	Hopkins, Lee Bennett	Harper & Row	10 or 11	M	2	Secondary
111. Secrets (1979)	Hopper, Nancy	Elsevior/Nelson	12	F	4	Incidental
112. Carrie's Games (1987)	Hopper, Nancy	Dutton	17	F	4	Secondary
113. Up A Road Slowly (1966)	Hunt, Irene	Follett	7-17	F	4	Secondary
114. Me and Mr. Stenner (1976)	Hunter, Evan	Lippincott	11	F	5	Central
115. Ollie's Go-Kart (1971)	Huston, Anne	Seabury	10	M	3	Central
116. Kim/Kimi (1987)	Irwin, Hadley	MacMillan	16	F	5	Secondary
117. The Taste of the Spruce Gum Tree (1966)	Jackson, Jacqueline	Little, Brown	10 or 11	F	5	Central
118. Cowgirl Kate (1950)	Johnson, Enid	Messner	17	F	3	Central
119. The Empty Chair (1978)	Kaplan, Bess	Harper & Row	9-11	F	5	Central
120. Witchery Hill (1984)	Katz, Welwyn Wilton	Atheneum	14	M & F	3	Incidental
121. The Son of Someone Famous (1974)	Kerr, M.E.	Harper & Row	16	M	3	Incidental
122. Love is a Missing Person (1975)	Kerr, M.E.	Harper & Row	14	F	3	Secondary
123. Alive and Starting Over (1983)	Klass, Sheila Solomon	Scribner's Sons	15	F	4	Incidental
124. To See My Mother Dance (1981)	Klass, Sheila Solomon	Scribner's Sons	13	F	3	Incidental
125. Ghost Island (1985)	Klaveness, Jan O'Donnell	Macmillan	15	F	4	Secondary
126. Mom, The Wolf Man and Me (1972)	Klein, Norma	Avon	11	F	4	Incidental
127. Breaking Up (1980)	Klein, Norma	Pantheon	15	F	4	Secondary

	Title	Author	Publisher	Age of [a]MC	Sex of [b]MC	Literary Quality [c]Rating	Stepfamily Theme
128.	Family Secrets (1985)	Klein, Norma	Dutton	18 & 17	F & M	5	Central
129.	Angel Face (1984)	Klein, Norma	Viking	15	M	5	Secondary
130.	Journey to an 800 Number (1982)	Konigsburg, E.L.	Atheneum	12	M	4-5	Incidental
131.	Hiding Places (1987)	Lachman, Lyn Miller	Stamp Out Sheep Square One Pub.	17	M	3	Secondary
132.	The Skating Rink (1969)	Lee, Mildred	Seabury	15	M	4	Incidental
133.	Isabel's Double (1984)	Lillington, Kenneth	Faber & Faber	16	M & F	4	Incidental
134.	Odd Girl Out (1978)	Lingard, Joan	Elsevier/Nelson	14	F	5	Central
135.	Strangers in the House (1981)	Lingard, Joan	Dutton	13 & 14	F/M	5	Central
136.	Switcharound (1985)	Lowry, Lois	Houghton Mifflin	13 & 12	M/F	3	Central
137.	The Un-Duddling of Roger Judd (1983)	Luger, Harriet	Viking	16	M	5	Central
138.	Dark but Full of Diamonds (1981)	Lyle, Katie	Coward, McCann & Geoghegan	16	M	4	Central
139.	Terror Run (1982)	MacKellar, William	Dodd, Mead	15	M	2-3	Incidental
140.	Sarah, Plain and Tall (1985)	MacLacklan, Patricia	Harper & Row Junior Books	School age up	F	3	Central
141.	Brother Enemy (1979)	Mace, Elizabeth	Beaufort	Young adult	M	3	Incidental
142.	Danny Rowley (1969)	Maddock, Reginald	Little, Brown	12	M	3	Central
143.	The Daughter of the Moon (1980)	Maguire, Gregory	Farrar, Straus, Giroux	12	F	3	Central
144.	The Abracadabra Mystery (1961)	Maher, Ramona	Dodd, Mead	14	F	4-5	Central
145.	Aliens in the Family (1985)	Mahy, Margaret	Scholastic	13 or so	F	5	Central
146.	The Changeover: A Supernatural Romance (1984)	Mahy, Margaret	Atheneum	14	F	3	Secondary
147.	The Impact Zone (1986)	Maloney, Ray	Delacorte	15	M	3 or 4	Central

Title	Author	Publisher	Age of [a]MC	Sex of [b]MC	Literary Quality [c]Rating	Stepfamily Theme
148. Trouble Half-Way (1985)	Mark, Jan	Atheneum	10-12	F	5	Central
149. Bummer Summer (1983)	Martin, Ann M.	Holiday House	12	F	5	Central
150. Missing Since Monday (1986)	Martin, Ann M.	Holiday House	15	F	2	Secondary
151. Guy Lenny (1971)	Mazer, Harry	Delacorte	12	M	3	Central
152. Hey Kid, Does She Love Me (1984)?	Mazer, Harry	Crowell	18-19	M	4	Secondary
153. The Dollar Man (1974)	Mazer, Harry	Delacorte	14	M	5	Incidental
154. Summer of the Zeppelin (1983)	McCutchen, Elsie	Farrar Straus Giroux	12	F	5	Secondary
155. Count Me In (1986)	McDonnell, Christine	Viking Penguin	14	F	5	Central
156. Hideaway (1983)	McGraw, Eloise	Atheneum	12	M	3	Secondary
157. Karen & Vicki (1984)	McHugh, Elisabet	Wm. Morrow	12	F	3	Central
158. Karen's Sister (1983)	McHugh, Elisabet	Greenwillow	11	F	2	Incidental
159. Tough Choices (1980)	Mendonca, Susan	Dial	14	F	4	Central
160. Nowhere to Run (1978)	Milton, Hilary	Franklin Watts	13	M	2	Secondary
161. Year of the Black Pony (1976)	Morey, Walter	Dutton	11	M	4	Secondary
162. Will the Real Renie Lake Please Stand Up? (1981)	Morgenroth, Barbara	Atheneum	16	F	5	Central
163. Silver Woven in My Hair (1977)	Murphy, Shirley R.	Atheneum	13-15	F	2-3	Central
164. Twink (1970)	Neufield, John	New American	16	F	4	Secondary
165. The Case of the Frightened Friend (1984)	Newman, Robert	Atheneum	11-12	F	2	Incidental
166. And Maggie Makes Three (1986)	Nixon, Joan Lowery	Harcourt, Brace, Jovanovich	12	F	4	Incidental
167. Where Do I Fit In? (1981)	Noble, June	Holt, Rinehart & Winston	5	M	5	Central

Title	Author	Publisher	Age of [a]MC	Sex of [b]MC	Literary Quality [c]Rating	Stepfamily Theme
168. Lillian (1968)	Norris, Gunilla B.	Atheneum	6 or 7	F	3	Incidental
169. Red Hart Magic (1976)	Norton, Andre	Crowell	Early adol.	F/M	4	Central
170. Girl Missing (1976)	Nostlinger, Christine	Franklin Watts	14	F	4	Central
171. Fair Game (1977)	O'Hanlon Jacklyn	Dial	14	F	1	Central
172. My Mother is Not Married to My Father (1979)	Okimoto, Jean Davies	Putnam's	11	F	3-4	Secondary
173. It's Just Too Much (1980)	Okimoto, Jean Davies	Putnam's	11 or 12	F	5	Central
174. A Formal Feeling (1982)	Oneal, Zibby	Viking	16	F	5	Secondary
175. One Step Apart (1978)	Oppenheimer, Joan L.	Grosset & Dunlap	16 & 17	M/F	3	Central
176. Gardine vs. Hanover (1982)	Oppenheimer, Joan	Crowell	15 & 16	F	3-4	Central
177. Last One Home (1986)	Osborne, Mary Pope	Dial	12	F	5	Central
178. Close Enough to Touch (1981)	Peck, Richard	Dell	16	M	4	Incidental
179. Telltale Summer of Tina C. (1975)	Perl, Lila	Clarion	12	F	3-4	Central
180. A Smart Kid Like You (1975)	Pevsner, Stella	Clarion	12	F	3-4	Central
181. Sister of the Quints (1987)	Pevsner, Stella	Clarion	13	F	3-4	Secondary
182. Marly the Kid (1975)	Pfeffer, Susan B.	Doubleday	15	F	1	Incidental
183. Starring Peter and Leigh (1979)	Pfeffer, Susan B.	Delacorte	16	F	3	Central
184. Our Family Got a Stepparent (1981)	Phillips, Carolyn E.	Regal	9 or 10	M	3	Central
185. A Tide Flowing (1981)	Phipson, Joan	Atheneum	10-15	M	4	Incidental
186. Cloris and the Creeps (1973)	Platt, Kin	Chilton	8 & 11	F	5	Central
187. Cloris and the Freaks (1975)	Platt, Kin	Bradbury	13 & 15	F	4	Central
188. Cloris and the Weirdos (1978)	Platt, Kin	Bradbury	13 & 15	F	4	Central

Title	Author	Publisher	Age of [a]MC	Sex of [b]MC	Literary Quality [c]Rating	Stepfamily Theme
189. The Ape Inside Me (1979)	Platt, Kin	Lippincott	15	M	3	Incidental
190. Rats, Spiders, & Love (1986)	Pryor, Bonnie	Wm. Morrow	11	F	4	Incidental
191. Who's Afraid (1980)	Rabe, Berniece	Dutton	16	F	2	Secondary
192. Nothing Stays the Same (1981)	Radley, Gail	Crown	12	F	3	Central
193. Pisces Times Two (1985)	Rees, E.M.	Putnam	16 or 17	F	2	Central
194. Three Wild Ones (1963)	Reese, John	Westminster	16	M	3	Incidental
195. The Journey Back (1976)	Reiss, Johanna	Crowell	12	F	4	Central
196. Apples Every Day (1965)	Richardson, Grace	Harper & Row	13	F	3	Incidental
197. Don't Hurt Laurie (1978)	Roberts, Willo D.	Atheneum	11	F	5	Secondary
198. Hiding Out (1974)	Rockwell, Thomas	Bradbury	9 or 10	M	3	Central
199. The Rare One (1973)	Rogers, Pamela	Thomas Nelson	13	M	3	Secondary
200. The Caretaker (1980)	Roth, Arthur	Four Winds	17	M	4	Incidental
201. The Secret Lover of Elmtree (1976)	Roth, Arthur	Fawcett Juniper	17	M	5	Incidental
202. What Do You Do In Quicksand? (1979)	Ruby, Lois	Viking	16/17	F/M	2	Incidental
203. Dance a Step Closer (1984)	Ryan, Mary E.	Delacorte	15	F	4	Secondary
204. Shyster (1985)	Sachs, Elizabeth Ann	Atheneum	10	F	4	Central
205. Secret Places of the Stairs (1984)	Sallis, Susan	Harper & Row	17	F	4	Secondary
206. An Open Mind (1978)	Sallis, Susan	Harper & Row	16	M	5	Central
207. Run, Shelley, Run (1974)	Samuels, Gertrude	Crowell	16	F	3	Incidental
208. Adam's Daughter (1977)	Samuels, Gertrude	Crowell	17	F	5	Secondary
209. The Young Barbarians (1947)	Sattley, Helen R.	Wm. Morrow	16	F	2-3	Secondary
210. Wait Until Tomorrow (1981)	Savitz, Harriet M.	Signet		M	4	Incidental

Title	Author	Publisher	Age of [a]MC	Sex of [b]MC	Literary Quality [c]Rating	Stepfamily Theme
211. North Star (1972)	Schraff, Ann	Macrae Smith	16	F	3	Secondary
212. Home is Where They Take You In (1980)	Seabrooke, Brenda	Wm. Morrow	12	F	3	Secondary
213. In the Castle of the Bear (1985)	Senn, Steve	Atheneum	12	M	5	Central
214. Too Much T.J. (1986)	Shannon, Jacqueline	Delacorte	16-17	F	3	Central
215. He Noticed I'm Alive . . . and Other Hopeful Signs (1984)	Sharmat, Marjorie Weinman	Delacorte	15	F	3	Incidental
216. Almost April (1956)	Sherburne, Zoa	Wm. Morrow	16	F	2	Incidental
217. Girl in the Mirror (1966)	Sherburne, Zoa	Wm. Morrow	16	F	5	Central
218. Don't Call Me Toad (1987)	Shura, Mary Frances	Dodd, Mead & Co.	11 (2)	F	3	Secondary
219. My Brother, the Thief (1980)	Shyer, Marlene F.	Scribners	12	F	5	Central
220. Libby's Step-Family (1966)	Simon, Shirley	Lothrop, Lee & Shepard	13	F	3	Central
221. Harper's Mother (1980)	Simons, Wendy	Prentice-Hall	14	F	3	Secondary
222. The Real World (1985)	Sirof, Harriet	Franklin Watts	15	F	4	Central
223. Fingers (1983)	Sleator, William	Atheneum (Bantam)	18	M	4	Incidental
224. Love and Tennis (1979)	Slote, Alfred	Macmillan	15	M	2	Incidental
225. Return to Bitter Creek (1986)	Smith, Alison	Viking Penguin	12	F	5	Secondary
226. A Trap of Gold (1985)	Smith, Doris Buchanan	Dodd, Mead	13	F	4	Incidental
227. Last Was Lloyd (1981)	Smith, Doris Buchanan	Viking	12	M	5	Incidental
228. The First Hard Times (1983)	Smith, Doris Buchanan	Viking	12	F	5	Central
229. Kick a Stone Home (1974)	Smith, Doris Buchanan	Crowell	15	F	5	Secondary
230. The Headless Cupid (1971)	Snyder, Zilpha K.	Atheneum	11	M	3	Central
231. Nobody's Brother (1982)	Snyder, Anne & Pelletier, Louis	New American Library	16	M	4	Central

Title	Author	Publisher	Age of [a]MC	Sex of [b]MC	Literary Quality [c]Rating	Stepfamily Theme
232. My Other-Mother, My Other-Father (1979)	Sobol, Harriet Langsam	MacMillan	12	F	4	Central
233. Lotte's Locket (1964)	Sorenson, Virgina	Harcourt, Brace, Jovanovich	9	F	3	Central
234. A Lemon and A Star (1955)	Spykman, E.C.	Harcourt, Brace, Jovanovich	4, 8, 10, 13	M/F; M/F	2	Incidental
235. The Wild Angel (1957)	Spykman, E.C.	Gregg	6, 9, 11, 14	M/F; M/F	4	Secondary
236. Terrible Horrible Edie (1960)	Spykman, E.C.	Harcourt, Brace & World	10	F	2	Secondary
237. Good-bye Glamour Girl (1984)	Tamar, Erika	Lippincott	10	F	3	Incidental
238. No Scarlett Ribbons (1981)	Terris, Susan	Farrar, Straus & Giroux	13	F	2	Central
239. I Double Love You (1985)	Tessler, Stephanie Gordon	Berkely Pub Group (Tempo Books)	17	F	2	Secondary
240. Changing of the Guard (1986)	Thomas, Karen	Harper & Row	16	F	5	Incidental
241. And Leffee was Instead of A Dad (1971)	Thorvall, Kerstin	Bradbury Press	9	M	5	Secondary
242. A Taste of Daylight (1984)	Thrasher, Crystal	Atheneum	16	F	4	Incidental
243. A Time to Fly Free (1983)	Tolan, Stephanie S.	Scribner's Sons	10	M	3	Incidental
244. Mary Louise and Josie O'Gorman (1922)	Van Dyne, Edith	Reilly & Lee	10-25	F	2	Secondary
245. None of the Above (1974)	Wells, Rosemary	Dial Press	13-18	F	5	Central
246. The Scare Crows (1981)	Westall, Robert	Greenwillow	13	M	4	Central
247. Life Without Friends (1987)	White, Ellen Emerson	Scholastic	18	F	5	Secondary
248. The Four Young Kendalls (1932)	White, Eliza Orne	Houghton Mifflin	14, 12, 9, 6	F/M; M/F	2	Central
249. A Sheltering Tree (1985)	Whitley, Mary Ann	Walker	13	F	5	Central

Title	Author	Publisher	Age of [a]MC	Sex of [b]MC	Literary Quality [c]Rating	Stepfamily Theme
250. Linda's Homecoming (1950)	Whitney, Phyllis	David McKay	16	F	4	Central
251. Storm from the West (1963)	Willard, Barbara	Harcourt, Brace, Jovanovich	6MC's	M/F	3	Central
252. Mitzi and Frederick the Great (1984)	Williams, Barbara	Dutton	8	M/F	5	Incidental
253. Mitzi's Honeymoon With Nana Potts (1983)	Williams, Barbara	Dutton	8	F	4	Central
254. Mitzi and the Elephants (1985)	Williams, Barbara	Dutton	8	F	4	Incidental
255. Mitzi and the Terrible Tyrannosaurus Rex (1982)	Williams, Barbara	Dutton	8	F	4	Central
256. Hey, What's Wrong With This One? (1969)	Wojciechowska, Maia	Harper & Row	7	M	3	Central
257. Out of Love (1976)	Wolitzer, Hilma	Farrar, Straus & Giroux	12 or 13	F	5	Central
258. Wish You Were Here (1984)	Wolitzer, Hilma	Farrar, Straus & Giroux	14	M	5	Secondary
259. Happily Ever After . . . Almost (1982)	Wolkoff, Judie	Bradbury	12	F	4	Central
260. Getting Rid of Marjorie (1981)	Wright, Betty Ren	Holiday House	11	F	4	Central
261. Ghosts Beneath Our Feet (1984)	Wright, Betty Ren	Holiday House	12	F	3	Secondary
262. The Summer of Mrs. MacGregor (1986)	Wright, Betty Ren	Random House	12	F	4	Incidental
263. Remember Me When I Am Dead (1980)	York, Carol Beach	Elsevier/Nelson	13	F	3	Incidental
264. Maybe It Will Rain Tomorrow (1982)	Zalben, Jane Breskin	Farrar, Straus Giroux	16	F	5	Central
265. My Darling, My Hamburger (1969)	Zindel, Paul	Harper & Row	17	F	3	Incidental

NOTE: [a]MC = Main Character   [b]F = Female   M = Male

[c]Literary Quality Rating 1-5 refers to the Literary Quality Scale in Chapter 3, page 32-33.

1 = no merit

2 = some merit

3 = average merit

4 = above average merit

5 = superior merit

BOOK SUMMARIES AND CODING

BOOK SUMMARIES AND CODING

Stepmother Stepfather	Stepsiblings # Sex	Stepfamily Formed Due to Death or Divorce	Summary	[d]Themes	Suggested Age Range of Readers	Recommended
1. SF	1 stepbrother 1 stepsister	Death	Stepsisters with very different personalities are jealous of each other at first but find they are actually complementary — like vanilla & chocolate. The ghost story aspect of the book is not plausible but the "real" characters reflect clinical impressions of stepfamily members.	a,f,h,j, l,o,t	11-16	Yes, highly
2. SM	1 stepbrother	Death	Jodi finds adjusting to a stepmother and brother difficult after having her father to herself for several years. However, she finds losing them worse.	e,g,h,k, n,p,s,t	11 up	Yes, highly
3. SF	0	Death	7 yr. old Lynette's mother drowns & her new stepfather is not sure what to do with her. An unusual friendship develops between Lynette & 12 yr. old Jeremy as they attempt to find her a home. Lynette resourcefully finds a home for herself.	g,m,n,s	11 up	Yes, highly
4. SM	0	Divorce	Anne thinks her boyfriend, Kyle, is the most wonderful boy she has ever met, despite the fact that no one in her family really approves of the relationship. Predictable story of a good girl going out with a wild boy & ending up disillusioned with him.	h,i,m,u	13-18	No
5. SF	3 half brothers	Death	Shy 13 yr. old Shari, abused at home by a mother who resents her, is befriended by a neighbor who shares her love of birds and outdoors.	m	11 up	Yes

Stepmother Stepfather	Stepsiblings # Sex	Stepfamily Formed Due to Death or Divorce	Summary	[d]Themes	Suggested Age Range of Readers	Recommended
6. SF	0	Divorce	When her parents decide to live apart, 11 yr. old Case tries to figure out a way to keep the family together so she doesn't have to separate from her beloved sister.	a,f,m,n,t		Yes, highly
7. SM	0	Divorce	After their father & stepmother were divorced, Lisa and her brother, Eric, wanted to live with their stepmother. Their father refused to let them, & their home life was very unhappy until they learned that children have legal rights.	a,g,l,m, q,r	12-16	Yes
8. SM	0	Divorce	After Duffy's father is killed in a car accident she becomes involved in a struggle between her biological mother who abandoned her as a baby & her stepmother whom Duffy had always thought was her biological mother.	a,d,e,g, n,q	10 up	Yes
9. SF	1 stepbrother	Death	Bernadette, whose father was killed in Vietnam, ends up asking her stepfather to adopt her so they'll all have the same last name in this tale of black magic and murder. Exciting plot in which it appears the stepbrother may have been involved in the murders.	a,g,h,l, n,r,t	11-16	Yes
10. SM	2 half-brothers	Death	Basically a book about an adolescent girl growing up & the way she deals with the death of a friend. Translated from Swedish.	no themes	14-17	No
11. SM	0	Death	Kirsty struggles with loyalty, jealousy, feeling displaced. When her younger brother suffers an injury she finds she is still needed & her relationship with her stepmother changes. The book contains a ghost story element also.	a,c,g,l, n,o,t	12 up	Yes
12. SM	1 stepsister 1 stepbrother	Abandoned	Heather's sophomore year brings many changes due to her father's tragic death. She becomes very involved with her boyfriend, Nicky, who is having problems with his stepmother.	b,c,d,e, g,h,m, n,p	11 up	Yes

Stepmother Stepfather	Stepsiblings # Sex	Stepfamily Formed Due to Death or Divorce	Summary	[d]Themes	Suggested Age Range of Readers	Recommended
13. SF	1 halfbrother	Not stated	Life at home hadn't been much for a long time for Patsy Bligh thanks to her stepfather. Her mother was tired all the time & her stepfather yelled at her, hit her & shamed her for wetting her bed. Patsy's only escape was to dream of her neighbor in Margate and life as it was with her mother before Eddie Green and the "baby." Finally she leaves &, in his journey to find her, Eddie Green learns something of himself. The story is trite & filled with odd characters.	g,s,r	11-14	No
14. SF	0	Divorce	When his stepfather abandons Tim and his mother, Tim must learn to cope with his loneliness & learn to deepen his relationship with those still close to him.	d,f,g	12-16	Yes
15. SF	2 step- brothers 1 stepsister	Death of ex- wife of stepfa- ther; MCs father was a drunk who abandoned the family when MC was one year old.	Merging of stepfamily and adoption of main character. Unrealistic situation comedy. Contrived happy ending with stepchild accepting stepfather and stepsibs.	b,d,e,g, h,n,o,p, t,u,a	9-12	Yes
16. SM/ SF	1 stepbrother	Death/Death	Two friends with 1 parent each decide to do some match-making, only to later wonder if they've been too successful. Fairly superficial story where all turns out predictably.	h,n,p	8-12	Yes
17. SM	0	Death	Stacy's mother, an alcoholic, left when Stacy was small. Stacy resents Barbara, her pregnant stepmother, runs away & is befriended by a wizened old woman who lives alone in the desert. Pat answers are not provided but the book is hopeful in tone.	a,g	10-15	Yes
18. SM	0	Death	Phillip has always lived with his grandmother, but when his father remarries he goes to London to live with his father and stepmother. Although he likes his stepmother, he finds out he doesn't like his father & neither does his grandmother.	a,m,n, q,u	10 up	Yes

Stepmother Stepfather	Stepsiblings # Sex	Stepfamily Formed Due to Death or Divorce	Summary	[d]Themes	Suggested Age Range of Readers	Recommended
19. SF	0	Death	On a visit to a country under rule of a dictator the children become involved in a revolutionary secret.	t	9-13	Yes
20. SF	0	Divorce	While the 13 yr. old Easterner Paul is visiting his grandmother in Colorado, she gives him a heart-decorated belt buckle that had belonged to a distant, vaguely remembered relative. Paul & his new friend, Jay Jenkins, a Ute Indian, hunt through dusty attic trunks & yellowing newspaper clippings trying to discover more about it's enigmatic owner and their search uncovers a more perplexing puzzle.	no themes	12-17	No
21. SM	0	Divorce	Amusing story set in New York. Incorporates typical concerns of young adolescent with adjustments from single parent (father) to remarried household. Stepmother's dog at first irritates Louise & then brings her in contact with a boy who never noticed her before. Overwritten in style and scope but provides some insight.	a,b,d,f, j,n,o,t	10-13	Yes
22. SF	0	Divorce	Julie misses her friends and biological father, is having trouble adjusting to stepfather, and feels she's a nuisance & an intruder in her new home.	b,d,e,g, m,n,o,s,t	11-14	Yes
23. SF	1 stepbrother 1 stepsister	Divorce	A young boy tries to come to terms with his mother's remarriage & his role as a stepchild. This story is illustrated with photographs on alternate pages. The writing is not at a difficult level & the book covers a large number of step issues in very few pages.	a,b,c,d, f,g,h,j, m,n,o,p, q,t	8-12	Yes

Stepmother Stepfather	Stepsiblings # Sex	Stepfamily Formed Due to Death or Divorce	Summary	[d]Themes	Suggested Age Range of Readers	Recommended
24. SF/ SM	1 half sibling 1 stepsib	Divorce	Avina has to deal with her two families (one week with one, the next week with the other), a new baby brother, a crush on an unattainable boy, and a troubled schoolmate who turns out to be a really good friend & strong support. She tolerates her stepparents who do "all the right things."	a,f,j,n,t	8-12	Yes
25. SM	1 stepbrother	Death	Catherine's journal, kept the last year she lived on the family farm, records her father's remarriage, which she resents somewhat, and the death of her best friend. Excellent portrayal of the times.	c,g,n,t	12-15	Yes
26. SM	1 stepsister 2 stepbrothers	Death	A mystery at Hadrians' Wall where the stepmother is an archaeologist. Melding 2 families with children is realistically handled.	b,h,m, p,t	12-16	Yes
27. SM	1 half brother	Abandonment	High school boys attempt to help beautiful suicidal cheerleader. It's inferred that Katie is suicidal because her mother abandoned her, and her stepmother is cruel and favors her own child. There is little development of characters & stepfamily life is presented extremely negatively.	e,m,s	14 up	No
28. SM	0	Death	Girl adjusts to new stepmother while continuing to aim at becoming a veterinarian like her father.	m,o	11-15	No
29. SM	1 half brother	Divorce	Dave's half-brother Jim joins Dave & his mother after their father dies. Jim has been in a rehabilitation center and gets in trouble again. Tragic ending.	b,e	12 up	No
30. SF	0	Divorce	A family who hits bottom. Cruel stepfather, mother who doesn't care, 18 and 17-yr-old brother and sister trying to hold things together for a 3- and 10-yr-old brother and sister.	b,i,k,m,s	14-17	No

Stepmother Stepfather	Stepsiblings # Sex	Stepfamily Formed Due to Death or Divorce	Summary	[d]Themes	Suggested Age Range of Readers	Recommended
31. SM	0	Death	Deals mainly with Rosie, a remarkable 10 yr. old, and her struggle with life including an actor father who decides to wed without telling her. Rosie's search for religion is also a theme.	a,e,g,m, n,u	10-13	Yes
32. SM/ SF	1 stepsister	Death	Story of a true "wicked" stepmother. The stepsisters are friends, however. Kate discovers her mother is jealous of her stepdaughter, Katherine, and is employing black witchcraft against her. Kates risks her own safety to protect her stepsister.	a,b,g,h, m,n,o, p,s	14 & up	No
33. SF	1 half-sister 2 half-brothers		A young reporter investigating the murder of a call girl, uncovers evidence that casts suspicion on his own half-brother. Depressing story of psychopathology. Set in England.	a	14 & up	No
34. SF/ SM	0	Divorce	Not actually a stepfamily book (the remarriage has not taken place). The dynamics, however, are those of a merging stepfamily. Two sisters look upon a beach vacation with their father, his woman friend, and her son, as 2 weeks in the wrong place with the wrong people. A near tragedy helps put things in perspective.	h,o,p,t	10-12	Yes
35. SM	3 half-sisters	Death	12 yr. old, Luvvy is the main character in this not very interesting book of family life in 1915. The title comes from the fact the father has 3 daughters from his 1st marriage (his 1st wife died) & 3 daughters, including Luvvy, from his current marriage. The story is about Luvvy's attempts to become one of "the girls" & leave her status as one of "the children."	h (½ sib relations)	10-12	No

Stepmother Stepfather	Stepsiblings # Sex	Stepfamily Formed Due to Death or Divorce	Summary	[d]Themes	Suggested Age Range of Readers	Recommended
36. SF	1 stepsister	Death	Convinced that his mother is dead after a car accident & unable to face life with his new stepfather, Robert runs into the Pine Barrens & engages in preposterous adventures of survival. Good adventure story.	no themes	12 up	Yes
37. Common law SF	0	Desertion	Drug abuse of main character & his adjustment to stepfather. Urban ghetto setting. Told from the point of view of several different characters.	b,r,t,u	12 up	Yes, highly
38. SM	1 stepsister	Death	1880's setting in an English vicerage; follows the life of Erica as she grows from 6-16 years of age. The relationship between Erica & her stepsister, Beatrice, is very uncomfortable. Beatrice is a pretentious genteel "wicked stepsister." Stereotypical situations, moral messages.	b,e,h	12-16	No
39. SF	0	Divorce	Kitty Dale, whose mother does not want to deal with a child, or admit one into her new life, spends the summer with Aunt Petal and eventually learns to accept her mother's weaknesses.	d,e,g, m,n	8-12	No
40. SF	0	Death	Insight into tumultuous feelings of a boy who, through his battle with a killer swan in order to protect a young cygnet he has adopted and his stepfather's quiet understanding, grows to see that he was not the cause of his father's suicide. Unusual book, brooding in tone.	d,g,l,n, r,t	12 up	Yes
41. SF	1 stepsister	Death	When Amy's mom remarries, it means moving from San Francisco to a guest ranch 300 miles away. Amy's stepdad gives her the summer to decide whether to stay or not. It is a tougher decision to make than she realized at first.	n,p	12 up	Yes

Stepmother Stepfather	Stepsiblings # Sex	Stepfamily Formed Due to Death or Divorce	Summary	[d]Themes	Suggested Age Range of Readers	Recommended
42. SF	0	Mother unmarried	Angie wants to meet her biological father (who doesn't know she exists) about whom she has fantasized. A story of a child trying to establish identity.	d	10 up	Yes
43. SM	0	Death	Samantha & her father have a very close and special relationship, which she feels is threatened when her father falls in love with Liz, a very special woman.	c,d,e,g, i,l,n,o	13-17	Yes, highly
44. SM	1 stepsister	Divorce	Amanda's comfortable practice of spending weekends with her divorced father is disrupted when he announces plans to remarry, providing her with a stepmother and stepsister her own age. Provides insight into why couples might divorce. Realistic dynamics.	a,b,e,g, h,j,m,n, o,p,t	12 up	Yes, highly
45. SF	0	Divorce	With her mother away on a honeymoon in Europe, 15 yr. old Darcie spends the summer with her dour uncle and his wife, restauranteurs in a zoo where Darcie begins a search for the father she has never known & develops a crush on a mysterious seal and bird keeper who leads her into a test with death.	g,n,o,u	12 up	Yes
46. SF	0	Divorce	A 15 yr. old & his divorced father become stranded and are offered refuge by a kind family in their farm house where they hear screams in the night, meet a threatening character, & eventually encounter vicious sheep thieves.	none	13 up	Yes, with reservations
47. SM	0	Death	When she arrives for a brief stay, 12 yr. old Theo has no idea how tied she is to Nantucket's past & how instrumental she will soon be in shaping the islands future. Entertaining ghost story although stepmother is immature and self-centered (but a minor character).	s,k	12-adult	Yes, with reservations

Stepmother Stepfather	Stepsiblings # Sex	Stepfamily Formed Due to Death or Divorce	Summary	dThemes	Suggested Age Range of Readers	Recommended
48. SF	0	Death	Adjusting to replacement of dead father with stepfather. Chris resents his mother's remarriage & has difficulty adjusting to his stepfather. When the stepfather buys "Smoke," a dog Chris found on the mountain, Chris realizes Cal is important to him & the family.	a,b,n,r,t	10-14	Yes
49. SF	0	Death	Entertaining but unlikely mystery involving 2 teenagers undergoing many changes in their lives.	r	11 and up	Yes
50. SF/ SM	0	Divorce	Bothered by her mother's & stepfather's drinking Di runs away to Calif. to see her father. On the road she gains self-discovery & decides she can't control others but can do something about herself.	d,k,m	13 up	Yes
51. SF	0	Divorce	This spy story is about Stephen Haden who smuggles people from behind the Iron Curtain to the West. An unexpected visit from his stepdaughter, Christa, interrupts an assassin who shot Stephen in the back and left him for dead. Haden becomes involved in a deadly game of double-cross in which Christa is the bait. He discovers he loves Christa enough to risk death for her. Interesting twist on stepfamily dynamics.	r	15 up	Yes
52. SF	0	Divorce	She started out as Janis May Finch, 17 yrs. old, living with her depressed mother, and trying to cope with a boring school & her mother's hostile boyfriend, Himmler. After another fight with her mother & Himmler, Janis steals 100 pds. and runs away to join Kelp, a rock band. Set in England.	m,o,b	14-18	No
53. SM	0	Death	A fairy tale with a magic bull set in Ireland.	no themes	8-10	No

Stepmother Stepfather	Stepsiblings # Sex	Stepfamily Formed Due to Death or Divorce	Summary	[d]Themes	Suggested Age Range of Readers	Recommended
54. SF	0	Divorce	Resentful of her parent's divorce, a young girl tries to accommodate herself to their new lives & also find a place for herself. Resents her impending stepfather and mother's values. Serious subject of divorce & joint custody blended with humor.	a,j,m	12 up	Yes
55. SM	2 stepbrothers 1 stepsister	Death	Unrealistic story with stereotypical wicked stepsister. Adjusting to school problems & the stepsister is the focus of this trite book.	h,n,p	9-12	No
56. SM	0	Death	Daughter of famous author is opposed to having a stepmother. Cornelia lives with the woman who ultimately becomes her stepmother while her father is in Brazil. Romantic, dated ridiculous plot.	d,n,o,r	12-16	No
57. SF	0	Divorce/ Abandonment	10 yr. old Angel finds plenty to worry about when she learns that her mother's new boyfriend is a clown. Nice story of a potential stepfather going slowly, making friends with the children, etc. Many things about the story are contrived, however.	n	7-10	Yes
58. SM/ SF	1 stepsister	Death/Divorce	6th grader, Philippa, feels her life becoming intolerable as her widowed father becomes romantically involved with a fellow architect, who is also the mother of Philippa's school enemy, Libby. Very little character development or insight.	a,b,h,n, o,p,u	8-12	Yes
59. SF	0	Unknown	Although grudgingly aware that 10 yr. old Pinkie has extraordinary power to heal, 16 yr. old Barry becomes increasingly convinced that she is an unwilling participant at the healing sessions run by her enterprising stepfather.	no themes	13-17	No

Stepmother Stepfather	Stepsiblings # Sex	Stepfamily Formed Due to Death or Divorce	Summary	[d]Themes	Suggested Age Range of Readers	Recommended
60. SM	0	Divorce	Davy's grandmother, with whom he's been living for years, dies, & all he has left is her house, his dog, and quarreling relatives. He goes to live in New York City with his semi-alcoholic mother, taking his dog—much to his mother's dismay. Davy is lonely, misses his grandmother & is totally mystifying to his mother. He gets along better with his stepmother and, to a lesser degree, his father. He attends a private boy's school & there are some overtones of homosexuality some might find objectionable. In some ways the book is more suited to adults.	e,g,j,k, m,n,o,u	12 up	Yes, with reservations
61. SF	0	Unknown	Katy is not looking forward to the changes her mother's marriage will bring. She fears her mother won't love her as much as her new husband.	o,m	4-8	Yes
62. SM	1 stepbrother 1 stepsister	Death	The main character discovered her stepfamily's sinister past & had to convince her father to leave in order for them to escape death at the hands of her stepmother. Involves witchcraft & evil stepmother.	d,g,h,i,p	12 up	No
63. SF	1 half-sister	Death/ Remarriage ended in Divorce	Tracy, a junior in high school, finds herself involved in a bizarre escapade designed to help 17 yr. old Brad "rescue" his half-sister from his former stepdad. Tracy learns that life is not black and white and that things are not always as they appear. Brad is a disturbed boy who has deluded himself into believing that his stepdad is the villain.	d,g,l,n	13 up	Yes

Stepmother Stepfather	Stepsiblings # Sex	Stepfamily Formed Due to Death or Divorce	Summary	[d]Themes	Suggested Age Range of Readers	Recommended
64. SM	1 stepsister	Death	Fanny & her stepsister are drawn into mysterious occurrences around their home in Scotland which seem to be connected to the unexplained disappearance of a young man in 1914. Good story of the occult. Realistic stepfamily portrayal.	h,t	12 up	Yes
65. SM	2 stepbrothers	Death	Liza, an only child, adjusts to her new stepfamily and a move to a small town in Washington. Her stepbrother, Steve, adjusts less well to the move, and his father leaving (he embezzled ½ million dollars and fled to Brazil). Steve does poorly in school and gets caught shoplifting. Realistic stepfamily dynamics.	a,b,d,h, n,t,p	12 up	Yes
66. SF	0	Unknown	3 sisters, abandoned by their mother and abusive stepfather, try to keep the truth from the neighbors and continue to operate the farm. Unrealistic story.	m,n,s,i	11 up	No
67. SF & SM	0	Divorce	Marcy longs for a father, becomes extremely attached to an elderly neighbor, and fantasizes he is her father.	a,d,f	10 up	Yes, highly
68. SF/ SM	1 stepsister 1 stepbrother	Divorce	Upset by her mother's remarriage, Marcy is upset further when she learns she'll be staying with her father whom she barely knows. Realistic portrayal of the difficulty of making adjustments in stepfamilies. Sequel to *A Private Matter*.	a,h,j,n, o,t	8 up	Yes, highly
69. SF	0	Divorce	Stepfather becomes infatuated with Laura, his stepdaughter. An unpleasant book that doesn't explain the characters' motivation for their behavior.	b,c,d,i, m,n,o,s	16 up	No
70. SF	0	Divorce	Dave runs away from his abusive loutish stepfather & intolerable home situation. Alcohol abuse, violence, & drug use are common in the book which ends tragically.	a,b,d,k, m,n,q,s	15 up	No

Stepmother Stepfather	Stepsiblings # Sex	Stepfamily Formed Due to Death or Divorce	Summary	[d]Themes	Suggested Age Range of Readers	Recommended
71. SM	1 stepsister 2 half brothers 1 half sister 1 stepbrother	Desertion followed by death	Bothered by a disinterested stepmother who fawns over her own child, Bonnie leaves school & attempts to find a job. Unable to do so, she re-thinks getting married and dropping out of school.	b	13-17	No
72. SM	0	Divorce	Preposterous, dated story of a girl desperately trying to get her parents back together after divorce.	f,g,l,n	15 up	No
73. SM	1 stepsister	Death	Entertaining but improbable mystery story of Cathy & her stepsister, Anne, who is at first presented as retarded & later revealed to be developmentally delayed due to emotional trauma. There is no friction in the stepfamily & few clues to how and why everyone adjusted so well.	h,m,n,p	9-12	Yes
74. SF	1 half-brother	Death	Erika has a hard time adjusting to Edvin her new stepfather, a baker, though her younger brother doesn't. Edvin is almost too good to be true in view of Erika's rejection of him. Edvin's niece and nephew help her adjust. Some (minimal) insight into living in Sweden.	a,d,n,t	12 up	Yes
75. SM	3 stepsisters	Death	Re-telling of the classical fairy tale of Cinderella.	b,h,p,s	8-12	No
76. SF	0	Death	Ibby's unhappiness at moving to Korea because of her new Army chaplain stepfather is alleviated when she meets new friends & solves a baffling mystery. Realistic situation of a surly adolescent making an entire family miserable.	a,d,n	11 up	Yes
77. SF	2 half-sisters	Death/Divorce	The plot actually deals with a situation in which the main characters **think** a stepfamily is going to be formed. The two families spend a holiday together on an island in the summer house of Ceecee's family. The dynamics of the 5 young people are similar to stepsibling dynamics.	a,f,h	14 up	Yes

Stepmother Stepfather	Stepsiblings # Sex	Stepfamily Formed Due to Death or Divorce	Summary	[d]Themes	Suggested Age Range of Readers	Recommended
78. SM	0	Divorce	Cory, the main character, does not live in a stepfamily but her best friend, Rachel Vellers, is living with her third stepmother. The story is one of understanding people's motives for behavior & being true to what you know is right. Insight into the reason for "snobbie-creepo" behavior on the part of 11 yr-old girls is given as well as insight into the behavior of divorced parents. Unfortunately, the stepfamily situation in the book is presented very negatively & Rachel is presented as a poor, neglected, suffering Cinderella (though she's not required to do any work!). The book mixes "fluff" & realism &, while it may appeal to young girls as entertainment, it could have been more.	j,m,s	9-12	Yes, with reservations
79. SM	0	Divorce	Funny, though improbable, story of Sport and his father who live in a dumpy apartment & Sport's rich mother who flits across Europe, sending Sport infrequent checks and making even less frequent visits. Sport's grandfather leaves 30 million dollars to him and now his mother wants him & goes to the extent of kidnapping him. A good picture of a kind and loving stepmother is presented.	m,q	10-12	Yes
80. SM	1 stepsister	Death	Sordid story of a stepfamily formed from the marriage of Robin's father to Liz's mother after Robin's mother & Liz's father were killed in a boating accident. Pete, Robin's older brother, is an alcoholic who flirts with his stepmother, Robin and Liz have intercourse during a storm after drinking 2 bottles of champagne and everyone feels guilty about the boating accident. Robin is a foodaholic.	h,i,k,l, p,s	16 up	No

Stepmother Stepfather	Stepsiblings # Sex	Stepfamily Formed Due to Death or Divorce	Summary	[d]Themes	Suggested Age Range of Readers	Recommended
81. SF	0	Death	Mrs. Abercorn, a retired writer of mysteries, takes 2 brothers under her wing during a difficult period in their lives & teaches them an unforgettable lesson in trust and friendship. Negative image of stepfamily.	g,k,m, n,s	10-14	Yes
82. SF	1 half-sister	Divorce	Told by Carrie, the 13 yr. old halfsister of Ben, who is presented as a "hippie." Thought provoking story of Ben's reunion with his father who left him at age six & whom he has not seen for at least 7 years. Somewhat, more superficially, the author deals with Ben's life with his stepfather, Carrie's father, who sends him messages through Carrie, & his mother who just worries about him. It is Carrie who seems to love him the most & who shares with Ben insight into human nature.	b,d,t	13 up	Yes
83. SF	0	Death	Victoria's mother is poor after the death of Victoria's father so they must move from Boston to a small village. Upset by the death of her father, economic restrictions, the move from Boston & the impending remarriage of her mother, Victoria becomes involved in a friendship with Hugh, a very powerful but nasty person.	a,n,	13 up	Yes
84. SM	1 stepbrother	Divorce	Adjusting to stepmother and stepbrother, & nursing a foal whose mother was killed by lightning, Kathy realizes she had misinterpreted her stepmother & stepbrother's motives & actions.	b,f,h,t	8-14	Yes
85. SF	1 stepsib 1 ½ sib	Death	After her mother's death 12 yr. old Babe begins to learn some hard truths about her mothers' life. Babe finds a nice family to take her in.	k,s	11-16	Yes
86. SM	0	Death	Migrant child searching for stability & roots. Good historical picture of the depression era.	t	10-13	Yes

Stepmother Stepfather	Stepsiblings # Sex	Stepfamily Formed Due to Death or Divorce	Summary	[d]Themes	Suggested Age Range of Readers	Recommended
87. SF/ SM	1 stepbrother	Divorce	An unrealistic, poorly developed story with no real message. Leslie must cope with her mothers' new life-style (she's reliving adolescence), her own relationships with two boyfriends, her fathers immaturity, & her stepsiblings ridiculous behavior. The stepfamily situation (father/stepmother) is a cartoon stereotype though Leslie will probably adjust well to her new mother/stepfather family.	h,j,m	13-16	No
88. SF	0	Divorce	Jess switches roles with her newly divorced mother who goes back to college & becomes a cheerleader. Silly story with some clinical themes. Family ends up in counseling. Jesse's father remarries.	n,f	11 up	Yes
89. SM? SF?	0	Polygamy	Danny's father becomes a Mormon & takes a second wife only 7 years older than Danny. After his father's death Danny's mother plans to remarry. Set in the 19th century.	a,d,e,f,g, k,m,n,r	15 up	No
90. SM/ SF	2 half-brothers	Divorce	Jenny went to live with her father in N.Y. To be accepted by her peers, she started using drugs with them, dating a drug dealer & became a heavy user.	b,d,h,j, m,n,o,q	12-17	Yes
91. SF	1 stepsister	Divorce	Casey sees few alternatives to negative behaviors & his poor adjustment to his parents divorce, his father's alcoholism, & his mother's remarriage leads him into fire setting behavior. After his dog, whom he talked to the world through, dies Casey burns down the family home & ends up in a detention center where he learns coping techniques and alternatives to his self-destructive reactive behavior. Realistic portrayal of therapy, "We're better than a family now—it looks as though we're on the way to being friends."	a,d,g,h,k	12 up	Yes, highly

Stepmother Stepfather	Stepsiblings # Sex	Stepfamily Formed Due to Death or Divorce	Summary	[d]Themes	Suggested Age Range of Readers	Recommended
92. SF	0	Divorce	Joshua's biological father is an undependable hippie from a wealthy family, & Joshua doesn't like the boyfriend his mother ultimately marries (even though the boyfriend in some ways buys him off). Family situations that would be painful (e.g., fights between Joshua & the soon-to-be-stepfather) are presented as funny. Flip language & many cliches.	d,n	12-16	No
93. SF	0	Death	Jane, her siblings, & mother move to Chapel Hill to be near her grandparents after the death of her father. Jane is opposed to her mother's re-marriage to the town doctor who was her "beau" before she married Jane's father. Everything turns out romantically & unrealistically well, how-ever, and the book ends at the beginning of the Civil War. Though well written, the book contains some objectionable material about slavery.	a,n	10-15	No
94. SF	0	Divorce	Paul is Rabbit, a shy boy with big ears who stutters. He lives with his grandmother and has waited for over 5 years for a call from his mother to tell him to come live with her, that she's found a bigger apart-ment, or a new husband who wanted him too. Paul decides finally he would rather live with his grandmother who loves and needs him.	a,d,m, s,u	10 up	Yes
95. SM	0	Divorce	The story centers on Al and her feelings, including those about her father whom she has not seen for 6 years and who suddenly gets in touch with her & wants her to come to his wedding. Shallow step-family plot but good character development. Though enter-taining, the book could have been considerably more. Al's	a,d	11-15	Yes

Stepmother Stepfather	Stepsiblings # Sex	Stepfamily Formed Due to Death or Divorce	Summary	[d]Themes	Suggested Age Range of Readers	Recommended
			anxiousness about attending her father's wedding & the possibility of her mother remarrying is treated too lightly.			
96. SM	0	Death	Mark, who feel's betrayed by his father's remarriage & who is the butt of some pranksters jokes, becomes filled with a hostility that permeates all his relationships & carries him into a near tragedy. Realistic book regarding stepfamily dynamics. Recommended for parents & adolescents.	a,g,i,o	11-15	Yes
97. SM	1 stepsister	Divorce	A young boy befriends his English stepsister. Shallow, unrealistic story about a boy who dreams of being a hero & then becomes one to his stepsister.	b,h,j,o,t	9-13	Yes
98. SM	3 stepbrothers	Divorce	In this sequel to *A Girl Called Al* and *I Know You, Al*, Al waits impatiently for a letter from the boy she met at her father's wedding and for a letter from Louise, her stepmother, inviting her to visit for a month in the summer. Told by her best friend, the story relays the agony of waiting to hear from someone, the difficulties of friendships & relationships, the misery of "rejection," the twinges of jealousy, & the sharing of true love. The book is funny, sad & fairly realistic.	a,d,j,l,t	10-15	Yes
99. SM	3 stepbrothers	Divorce	A sequel to *I Know You Al* & *Your Old Pal, Al*, this story is again told by Al's best friend. Al is now waiting excitedly to go visit her father, stepmother, stepbrothers, & "his boy" in the country. Her best friend is feeling sorry for herself because she isn't getting to go anywhere & everyone else will be out of town. Then calamity strikes, & Al can't go. What happens next to both her & her friend turns out to be much more important.	a,j,l,o,t	11-15	Yes

Stepmother Stepfather	Stepsiblings # Sex	Stepfamily Formed Due to Death or Divorce	Summary	[d]Themes	Suggested Age Range of Readers	Recommended
100. SF	0	Death	14 yr. old Samantha has difficulty coping with her mother's impending remarriage & tries to evade the situation by involving herself completely in the activities of the swimteam.	n	11-13	Yes
101. SF	0	Unclear (divorced or never married)	A lonely young girl develops such an intense attachment to a neighbor's dog that everyone else in her life takes second place. Set in England, the story has many interesting characters.	r	9-14	Yes
102. SF/ SM	1 stepsister	Desertion/ death	Molly and Michael dislike their new stepsister, Heather, but realize they must try to save her when she seems ready to follow a ghost child to her doom. Heather accidentally caused her mother's death in a fire & is keeping it a secret so everyone won't hate her.	b,g,h,l, n,o,p	9-15	Yes
103. SF	0	Never-married	17 yr. old Callie longs to help a trouble-prone young man, but she finally comes to realize some people cannot be changed. A book with a realistic, unromantic approach to life.	m,r,s	11 up	Yes, highly
104. SF	0	Death	Filled with violence, hatred and anger, the message conveyed by this book is one of despair and confusion. The picture portrayed of a stepson/stepfather relationship is very negative & the portrayal of the parallel nuclear family is no better.	b,g,l,m,s	10 up	No
105. SF	1 half-brother	Death	Main character is not a stepchild. She is babysitting with a 4 yr. old child who has a half brother. 4 yr. old Abby's mother is mentally unstable & kidnaps Abby while Erin is babysitting (Abby's father is away on business). With the help of Abby's half-brother, Dan, she is found & her mother falls to her death. Not recommended as a stepfamily book but a good adventure story.	m,q,s	13 up	No

Stepmother Stepfather	Stepsiblings # Sex	Stepfamily Formed Due to Death or Divorce	Summary	[d]Themes	Suggested Age Range of Readers	Recommended
106. SF	1 stepbrother	Divorce	Wedge, an overweight, lonely, unhappy child is torn with his illusions about his absent biological father & the presence of his new stepfather, stepbrother and expected half-sibling. His mother is presented in a much less favorable light than the rescuing stepfather. Happy ending is unrealistic & much too soon to be plausible.	d,h,n,p,r	8-11	Yes
107. SF	2 half sisters	Divorce	Charles is surrounded by women — his older half-sister whom he feels hates him, his mother whom he feels puts up a shield when his older sister is around, & his younger half-sister whom he gets along with. He has had 3 stepfathers & thinks his mother is angling for a fourth. Charles deliberately fails the entrance to a private boys' boarding school because he thought his sister was going away to school. When he finds out she's not, he seeks out a tutor, the man without a face. Some may object to the references to homosexuality, however, the book is well written and thought provoking.	d,h	14 up	Yes
108. SM	1 stepbrother	Divorce, though main character was told her mother died.	Cathy learns about her relationship with others while spending the summer with her grandmother. She meets her biological mother whom she thought was dead, conquers her fear of animals & her need to be number 1 in all important relationships.	h,k,m, p,u	10 up	Yes
109. SF/ SM	0	Divorce	After years of living with her mother, stepfather & their friend in Europe, Mopsy's mother suddenly wants her to meet her father whom she has never known and has grown to hate due to her mother's stories. She learns her father	a,d,g	15 up	Yes

Stepmother Stepfather	Stepsiblings # Sex	Stepfamily Formed Due to Death or Divorce	Summary	[d]Themes	Suggested Age Range of Readers	Recommended
			not only guessed at her existance (Mopsy's mother did not tell her father she was pregnant when she left him) & was afraid to see her, but that he is also an Episcopal priest and has remarried. When Mopsy's mother dies she is desolate but does not mourn. She goes to the United States to live with her father & kind stepmother and becomes very depressed until a special package arrives. Entertaining and deals with many issues of life and relationships.			
110. SF	0	Divorce	Pointless story of two young boys in lower SES single parent home. A few clinical insights from the school "psychiatrist" thrown in at the end.	o,n	9-12	No
111. SF	0	Death	Lenore, severely traumatized after witnessing her father's death, is not believed when she reveals to her psychiatrist and her English teacher that she and a classmate are targeted for kidnapping.	g,l,m,n,o	12 up	Yes
112. SM	0	Death	Thinking she can keep her widowed father from marrying a young woman, 17 yr. old Carrie begins a dangerous game of juggling 2 boyfriends.	g,l,m,n,o	15-18	Yes
113. SM	0	Death	A girl's maturation from age 7-17, her growing love for the maiden aunt who raises her and her adjustment to life changes (mother's death, father's remarriage, sister's marriage).	a,g,u	10 up	Yes
114. SF	2 stepbrothers	Divorce	Excellent humorous & realistic story of a young girl torn by loyalty conflicts, her embarrassment because her mother is cohabiting, & other typical problems associated with divorce & remarriage. Good portrayal of stepfamily dynamics; all characters are shown to have strengths & weaknesses.	a,j,n,t	11 up	Yes, highly

Stepmother Stepfather	Stepsiblings # Sex	Stepfamily Formed Due to Death or Divorce	Summary	[d]Themes	Suggested Age Range of Readers	Recommended
115. SF	0	Death	Relationship between Ollie, stepfather, & neighborhood boys. Ollie tries to adjust to SF who makes him feel stupid by his unrealistically high expectations.	b,n	10 up	No
116. SF	1 half-brother	Death	Despite a warm relationship with her mother, stepfather, & half brother, 16 yr. old Kim feels the need to find answers about the Japanese American father she never knew.	d,g	12 up	Yes
117. SF	0	Death	Turn of the century story of girl jealous about sharing mother with new stepfather (her father's brother). The setting is a lumber camp on the West Coast.	a,g,n,o,t	10 up	Yes
118. SM	0	Death	Soon after his remarriage to Ilsa (from New York City) Kate's father is killed by a wild horse he was breaking for Kate. His dying words to Ilsa are to look after Kate who was furious about the remarriage and has been obnoxious to Ilsa. A dated book in many ways, full of cowboy jargon, stereotyped characters & unrealistic romantic solutions to problems.	a,g,n,o	12-15	No
119. SM	0	Death	When Becky's mother dies while having an eagerly anticipated baby (the baby dies too—the story is set in 1930's), Becky is desolate. She is unable to accept the finality of the death & her new, very nice, stepmother even though she wants to.	a,d,g,l, n,r,t	10 up	Yes
120. SM	0	Death	Summering with his father on the channel Island of Guernsey, 14 yr. old Mike perceives inexplicable, but undeniable, signs of witchcraft which seem directed at destroying his friends. Mike's father is shallow & story is filled with violent, ugly characters.	s	12-16	No

Stepmother Stepfather	Stepsiblings # Sex	Stepfamily Formed Due to Death or Divorce	Summary	[d]Themes	Suggested Age Range of Readers	Recommended
121. SM	0	Death	Adam comes to live with his grandfather after being expelled from yet another private school. His father is very famous & Adam uses his mother's name trying to pretend to be the son of no one famous. He becomes friends with the town tomboy.	d,n	14-17	No
122. SM	0	Divorce	A dated 60's story of wealthy "liberal" White adolescent, Chicago, who goes through all the motions of being "free" — dress style, riding a motorcycle, dating a Black superstar and getting him involved in "causes." Some of this is in rebellion against her father whom she lived with until his remarriage. The characters are not well-developed nor is there much explanation offered for their behavior.	d,j,m,o	15 up	No
123. SM	0	Divorce	Peter, a hemophiliac, Martha, Jess's new stepmother, Sylvia, whose new stepmother made her have a "nose job," Brookie & Jason, & Jess's grandmother, who becomes ill, populate this interesting but somewhat trite book focused on changes in an adolescent's life.	n,t,u	11 up	Yes
124. SM	0	Divorce	13 yr. old Jessica longs for the mother who abandoned her as a baby & allows her fantasy of a perfect natural mother to color her attitude toward her father's new wife. Book presents all adults with the exception of Martha, the new stepmother, in a bad light. Shows good & bad aspects of stepmothers.	d,e,k,m, n,o,r,s	10 up	Yes
125. SF	0	Death	When Delia returns to the Canadian lake where her family had vacationed, she finds things greatly changed from the happy times of her childhood. Poachers endanger the local wildlife, her memories, & the lives of her family.	a,c,d,g, n,t	12-16	Yes

Stepmother Stepfather	Stepsiblings # Sex	Stepfamily Formed Due to Death or Divorce	Summary	[d]Themes	Suggested Age Range of Readers	Recommended
126. SF	0	Mother was never married	Brett doesn't want to share her mother with a stepfather; she fears changes in their relationship.	a	12 up	Yes
127. SM	0	Divorce	While visiting her father & stepmother in California, Alison learns her mother is a lesbian. The mother is presented as nearly perfect while the father and stepmother (a psychiatrist) don't come off well. The biological parents are still fighting over custody of the children. Though perhaps realistic, the presentation of sexual relations as "the thing to do" among 15 year olds seems unnecessarily blatant.	a,j,m,q	14 up	Yes, with reservations
128. SF/ SM	Each MC is the other's stepsibling.	Divorce	Peter (18) and Leslie (17), high school seniors, have to make some adjustments when Peter's father & Leslie's mother marry, making them stepbrother & stepsister. Interesting characterization of adults, none are perfect though some are more admirable than others.	a,h,i,m, n,p,s	14-18	Yes, with reservations
129. SF	1 sister 1 brother	Divorce	After his father walks out on his slightly crazy mother, 15 yr. old Jason, the last child at home, finds it difficult to deal with his mother's increasing desperation.	a,c,j,m,n	15 up	Yes, with reservations
130. SF	0	Divorce	When Maximillian Stubb's mother remarries and goes on a month long honeymoon cruise, she sends her son to stay with his father whom he has seen only once a year since he was 4. Max's father is a camel keeper who travels the country, showing his camel. Max doesn't like the fact his father keeps a camel nor that he lives a less than first class life. However, over the course of the month, Max learns a lot about life, people, his father, &, most of all, himself.	n	12 up	Yes

Stepmother Stepfather	Stepsiblings # Sex	Stepfamily Formed Due to Death or Divorce	Summary	dThemes	Suggested Age Range of Readers	Recommended
131. SF	0	Divorce	When living with his abusive stepfather becomes unbearable, 17 yr. old Mark tries unsuccessfully to commit suicide, then runs away to New York City where he encounters new problems living on his own.	b,d,g,k, m,n	15 up	Yes, with reservations
132. SM	2 half brothers 1 half sister	Death	Adolescent male overcomes low self-esteem & stuttering problem by becoming a skating star. The setting is rural Georgia and the problems are those of low income people with poor communication skills.	h,p,t	11-15	Yes
133. SF	0	Divorce	16 yr. old Mike & Isabel are characters in a ghost story. Stepfamily is incidental, in fact, as it turns out, the SF is actually the biofather. Isabel has a double who sometimes appears to her and also appears to Mike when the two are at a summer art school. Jenny, a teacher at the school, is a medium and helps solve the problem with the double.	l	13 up	Yes
134. SF	0	Divorce	Ellen, already troubled by her height (5'11"), finds life even more difficult when her mother decides to remarry. Ellen had been told her father, a pianist, was dead, and she revered his memory. Herbert, the stepfather, is a patient unexciting man who had been under his mother's thumb until her recent death. He and Ellen are both struggling with autonomy, and Herbert, in nonspectacular ways, does things well in attempting to help Ellen adjust to change.	a,d,e,n, t,g	13 up	Yes
135. SM/ SF	2 stepsisters 1 stepbrother	Divorce/death	A complex stepfamily in Scotland; money is tight & they are in crowded apartment. Colum is resentful of leaving the country, fishing, his friends & his father. Stella resents having to share her room with	a,d,e,h	12 up	Yes, highly

Stepmother Stepfather	Stepsiblings # Sex	Stepfamily Formed Due to Death or Divorce	Summary	[d]Themes	Suggested Age Range of Readers	Recommended
			Betsy, her father's attention, & her best friend who becomes Colum's girlfriend. All adults & children in the book are shown to have strengths & weaknesses. There are no villians, no heroes, only people struggling to work things out.			
136. SF	2 stepsibs	Divorce	Feuding siblings Caroline & J. P. Tate agree to call a truce in their personal warfare when a threat to their combined well-being rises. Their father, whom they haven't seen in years, wants them to spend the summer with him. Upon arrival, JP finds himself the coach of a baseball team made up of a motley crew of 6 yr. olds. Caroline has to share a room with six month old twins. Feeling unjustly afflicted, the two team up to plot the Tate Conspiracy for revenge.	j,l,m,n	10-13	Yes
137. SM	1 stepsister	Divorce	16 yr. old Canadian Roger, unhappy with himself and his life since his father's remarriage, goes to visit his mother, a recovered alcoholic, in New York City, where he has a revelation that changes his life. Realistic but stressful stepfamily environment.	a,b,d,e, h,k,m,n, o,p,s,t	12 up	Yes
138. SM	0	Death	In love with the woman his father also loves, Scott has trouble accepting their impending marriage. Explores many themes of growing up as well as some stepfamily themes.	d,g,i	14 up	Yes, with reservations
139. SF	0	Death	Hard-to-believe adventure story set in Scotland. Mark accompanies his stepfather, who is a U.S. intelligence agent, on a mission so that "they can get to know each other better." Mark misses his father & resents his stepfather's unwillingness to open up to him & tell him what he is up to.	a,c	14 up	No

Stepmother Stepfather	Stepsiblings # Sex	Stepfamily Formed Due to Death or Divorce	Summary	[d]Themes	Suggested Age Range of Readers	Recommended
140. SM	0	Death	When their father invites a mail-order bride to come to live with them in their prairie home, Caleb and Anna are captivated by her & hope she will stay. Period piece with little relevance for modern stepfamilies.	r,t	6-10	Yes
141. SF	1 half-brother	Divorce	The account of Andreaus Haussman, a Jewish immigrant to England during World War II. The book chronicles Andreaus's life in foster homes, his struggle to learn English, & his activities in school. Following the war's end, he returns to Germany to find his family. His father died in an immigration camp in England, his mother was killed for being a Jewish sympathizer & his half-brother had decided to hate him. A book about identity building although the psychological portrayal of Andreaus could have been better.	no themes	14 up	No
142. SF	1 F	Death	Danny hates his father's death, hates his mother remarrying, hates everything & gets in trouble with the law because of it.	a,b,d,h, o,p	11-15	Yes
143. SM	0	Divorce	Erikka lives in a small apartment in Chicago with her younger siblings, her stepmother & her traveling salesman father, surrounded by ugliness and people who are so caught up in day-to-day life they seem incapable of seeing beauty. Erikka can find peace in only one place — Tolyukov's bookstore — & now it appears it will close. Erikka enlists the aid of others to help her & learns something of herself in the process. The story also contains a magical quality; Erikka travels by means of a magic candlestick from Old Russia & a beautiful watercolor to another place.	d,e,g,n	10-14	Yes

Stepmother Stepfather	Stepsiblings # Sex	Stepfamily Formed Due to Death or Divorce	Summary	[d]Themes	Suggested Age Range of Readers	Recommended
144. SF	1 stepsister 1 stepbrother	Death	Jeanette & her mother move from Dallas to Santa Fe after her mother remarries. Jen is anxious to meet her new family, 15 yr. old Ted and 14 yr. old Torrey. The new stepfamily begins to mesh quite well except for Torrey who remains stubbornly loyal to the memory of her deceased mother. The mystery of the title revolves around a legacy left for Ted and Torrey by their maternal grandfather. Step themes are presented realistically for the most part.	d,h,p,t	13 up	Yes
145. SF & SM	1 stepsister 1 stepbrother	Divorce	Science fiction theme. Jake feels like an alien in her dad's new home. Shortly after her first visit has begun, Bond, an extraterristrial alien, is "saved" from capture by Dora. The theme of being in a new and strange culture is well-developed. Characters are realistically portrayed.	d,h,j,m, n,p,t,u	12-17	Yes
146. Doesn't apply	1 brother	Divorce	No one knew about what was ailing Laura's little brother, Jacko. Only she knew that he was dying because of a strange, unnatural possession. She alone was capable of saving him, but first she must make a "changeover" with the help of Sorry Carlisle, an older boy whose mother and grandmother were reputed witches. Other changes facing Laura included her mother's new male friend & her own relationship with Sorry.	a,d,i,m, n,o	14 up	No
147. SF	0	Divorce	While trying to deal with his parents' marital fortunes & his own burgeoning sexuality, Jim runs off to Hawaii where he courts death by riding the Banzai Pipeline (a surfing wave). None of the characters are especially appealing. Sexuality is presented as exploitive, parents allow 15 yr. olds to drink, etc.	a,d,i,m,s	14-18	No

Stepmother Stepfather	Stepsiblings # Sex	Stepfamily Formed Due to Death or Divorce	Summary	[d]Themes	Suggested Age Range of Readers	Recommended
148. SF	0	Death	Driving through England with her stepfather, Amy gains a new view of herself, her relationship with him, and the country through which she is traveling. Richard loosens her up & gives her opportunities to be independent and gain self-esteem.	a,n,r,t	12 up	Yes, highly
149. SM	1 stepsister 1 stepbrother	Death	Kammy has enjoyed her lifestyle living alone with her father since her mother died (when Kammy was 4) & resents all the adjustments she has to make when her father remarries a woman with a 3 yr old and a 2 month old baby. Having a young child & a baby in the house make life difficult for Kammy. In fact, a great deal of change and adjustment is required for everyone. A summer at Camp Arrowhead helps Kammy put her home life in perspective. Stepfamily dynamics are presented very realistically — a good picture of the early transition period.	h,m,n,o, p,t	10 up	Yes, highly
150. SM	1 half sister	Divorce	When their little sister doesn't come home from school, 15 yr. old Maggie & her brother must face up to some deep, dark secrets about their natural mother, who has kidnapped Courtney.	a,d,s	12-16	No
151. SF(SM)	0	Divorce	Lenny feels his father is growing away from him due to his new love — Emily. Suddenly, after 7 years Lenny's mother appears & wants him back. Lenny doesn't know what to think. He is left in a depressing no-win situation.	e,g,m, s,q	12 up	No
152. Doesn't apply	0	Doesn't apply	Jeff, the main character, falls in love with a single parent mother (Mary) & her baby daughter. The problem is Mary does not return his love. When	e,i,l,o,r	12 up	Yes

Stepmother Stepfather	Stepsiblings # Sex	Stepfamily Formed Due to Death or Divorce	Summary	[d]Themes	Suggested Age Range of Readers	Recommended
			he offers to take care of her baby for a weekend he thinks it will bring Mary around to loving him.			
153. SF	0	(Mother never married but is living with Bill)	Raised by his mother, a fat 14 yr. old feels he must find his father in order to establish his identity. Good example of a child idealizing an unknown father.	d	12 up	Yes
154. SM	1 half brother	Death	1918 English village setting. Elvie's father is missing in action in France and she is living with her stepmother and half brother. Elvie and Clarry Rae, an orphan boy, find an abandoned house they plan to run away to (Elvie thought her SM only cared about her Dad & half sib). Bill, a German prisoner, also finds the house & he and Elvie become friends.	t	10-16	Yes
155. SF	1 ½ sib	Divorce	13 yr. old Katie has a difficult time adjusting to her new family situation, especially after her mother & new stepfather announce that they are expecting a baby. Katie at first felt left out & missed having special times with her mom but after a couple years the stepfamily adjusts.	m,n,t, u,o	10-16	Yes, highly
156. SF	2 stepsisters 1 stepbrother	Divorce	Jerry, anxious about what life will be like with a new stepfather and stepsiblings, runs away to his grandparents' house only to find out they don't live there anymore. He develops a relationship with Hanna, a foster child, who is taking care of the house while the occupants are on vacation.	d,n	11 up	Yes
157. SF/ SM	3 stepsibs, expecting a ½ sib	Adopted by single mother/ death	When Karen's mother marries, Karen must learn to adapt to living with a complete family, & in particular with her older step-sister, Vicki.	b,e,h,n, o,p,t,u	8-12	Yes

Stepmother Stepfather	Stepsiblings # Sex	Stepfamily Formed Due to Death or Divorce	Summary	[d]Themes	Suggested Age Range of Readers	Recommended
158. SF	3 stepsibs	Mother never married	Second book in a trilogy. Karen's mother adopts a second Korean child & at the end of the book announces she is marrying a man with 3 children.	n,u	10-12	Yes
159. SM	1 half-sister	Divorce	Crystal has to choose between living with her unreliable mother or living with her father, his new wife and daughter. Sad book about a girl torn between her parents. Originally choosing her mother because she doesn't think her mother can survive without her, Crystal later decides to live with her father. Fitting into the stepfamily proves harder than she thought because she's not used to responsibility and discipline. Stepfamily dynamics not well developed.	a,d,h,j,n	12-15	Yes
160. SM	0	Divorce	Wayne and Linda live with their alcoholic mother who does little except sleep, eat, and go out. For years, even before their parents divorced, they had endured abuse from their mother. When their father arrives unexpectedly and invites them on a vacation they jump at the chance & only vaguely question the fact that their mother didn't mention it. They discover their father has only taken them to avoid high alimony and child support payments & that their stepmother wants nothing to do with them. They run away and become engaged in a series of misadventures as they head toward their grandfather's home.	k,q,s	13-15	No
161. SF	0	Death	Mainly about a horse, second family relationship. Set in the 1800s.	m,p,r	13-17	Yes

Stepmother Stepfather	Stepsiblings # Sex	Stepfamily Formed Due to Death or Divorce	Summary	[d]Themes	Suggested Age Range of Readers	Recommended
162. SM	1 half sib 3 stepsibs	Divorce	Following her parents' divorce, Renie falls in with bad company & experiences arrest, a new home, & mistreatment from her stepsister before she finally takes a stand against more trouble. Renie's friendship with Jan, a deaf boy, adds interest.	b,h,m,n, o,p,q,s,t	12 up	Yes
163. SF	2 stepsisters	Death	A fairytale with a wicked stepmother & 2 wicked stepsisters, similar to Cinderella.	s	13-17	No
164. SM- SF	1 stepbrother 3 stepsisters	Death	The story of Twink and her handicap as seen through the eyes of her stepbrother, Harry, & her older sister.	h	13-17	Yes
165. SM	0	Death	Andrew & Inspector Wyatt help a friend whose father has mysteriously died, whose grandfather is a complete invalid & who has reason to suspect his stepmother of wrong-doing.	s,u	9-12	No
166. SM	0	Death	12 yr. old Maggie, living with her grandmother in Houston, joins the drama club at school, wins a part in a play, begins to make friends, & learns to deal with feelings of loneliness, selfishness, being in love, & having an unusual family life & background.	d,m,n,u	10-14	Yes
167. SF	expecting a half-sib	Divorce	John's mother & stepfather are expecting a baby & John is not sure how he will fit into the family, especially with his stepgrandparents. His stepgrandparents make it very clear to John they consider him their grandson.	a,n,o,u	4-7	Yes
168. SF	0	Divorce	Lillian is afraid her mother will stop loving her as her father had stopped loving her mother (Lillian never sees her father after the divorce). Lillian slowly becomes more secure. Translated from Swedish.	d,m,n	7-11	Yes

Stepmother Stepfather	Stepsiblings # Sex	Stepfamily Formed Due to Death or Divorce	Summary	[d]Themes	Suggested Age Range of Readers	Recommended
169. SF/ SM	Each MC is the other's stepsibling	Death	Told from the two points of view (each main character) in two time periods (the present & ancient England). Youngsters who barely know their own parents are now stuck with each other at "Aunt" Elizabeth's. Nan has lived with her grandmother; Chris with various relatives, & both their parents had traveling jobs. They don't like their new school, the stepsibling situation, or Aunt Elizabeth. The problem is resolved through the mystery of the Red Hart Inn, an antique model Chris purchased at a Salvation Army store. Chris and Nan both have the same dreams about the Inn. Good fantasy with some insight into the problems of the two children.	h,m,n	12 up	Yes
170. SF	1 stepmother 1 stepfather	Divorce	Ilse runs away. Her sister finds out why and tells the story of her family at the same time. Translated from German.	b,m,u	12 up	Yes
171. SF	0	Divorce	14 year old Denise hates her stepfather—is deathly afraid of him because of his overt sexual actions toward her & his drinking. Because of her mother's and sister's seeming nonnoticing she feels she is going crazy. Her grades slip; she loses her best friend.	c,k,s	14 up	No
172. SF	2 stepbrothers	Divorce	Primarily the story of a young girl's adjustment to her parent's divorce & subsequent dating of other people. The idea of stepfamily relations are introduced in the end but the idea of divided loyalties is presented throughout.	a,g,j,l, m,o	10 up	Yes
173. SF	2 stepbrothers	Divorce	Cynthia has the usual problems of any 6th grader—her best friend is maturing and "turning beautiful," the boy down the street is a pest and	a,g,d,h,j, m,n,p,t	10 up	Yes

Stepmother Stepfather	Stepsiblings # Sex	Stepfamily Formed Due to Death or Divorce	Summary	[d]Themes	Suggested Age Range of Readers	Recommended
			she's getting a stepfamily—a new stepfather and two step-brothers (who will be around part-time) who seem to eat all the best food & who never have to follow the same rules. Cynthia's mother is sensitive to her needs, the stepbrothers decide that it isn't fair to anyone that they don't all have the same rules; & Cynthia learns that people can disagree and still love each other. Sequel to *My Mother Is Not Married to My Father.*			
174. SM	0	Death	Anne has not allowed herself to grieve for her mother or to view her mother realistically. Learns to accept fact that there are some things you have no control over.	d,g,n	12 up	Yes, highly
175. SM/ SF	2 half brothers 1 half sister 1 stepbrother	Divorce	Impending second divorce & friction between stepbrother and stepsister's boyfriend. Strong stepsibling relations portrayed.	h,p,t	12 up	Yes
176. SM/ SF	1 stepsister 1 stepbrother	Divorce	Jill's parents have divorced for seemingly no reason. Her mother is remarrying a man Jill sees as "her mother's husband" and with him are coming his 2 children, Carolyn and Drew, whom he hasn't lived with since his divorce. His children feel rejected by their mother, particularly Carolyn. Drew & Abby (Jill's sister) get along well but Carolyn and Jill don't. Their fighting eventually splits the marriage apart until illness miraculously brings everyone together again.	d,e,h,n, p,s,t	12 up	Yes
177. SM	0 Will soon have 2 stepsiblings	Divorce	12 yr. old Bailey struggles with her feelings of loneliness after her parents' divorce when her father plans to remarry & her brother prepares to leave for the service. Her alcoholic mother plays important role as Bailey mourns her "fantasy family."	a,b,d,g, h,k,n,o,t	10-15	Yes, highly

Stepmother Stepfather	Stepsiblings # Sex	Stepfamily Formed Due to Death or Divorce	Summary	[d]Themes	Suggested Age Range of Readers	Recommended
178. SM	0	Death	Matt's girlfriend suddenly and unexpectedly dies of a brain aneurysm & he must work through the grieving process.	a,c,g,r,u	13-16	Yes
179. SF	0	Divorce	Already unsure of herself, Tina is thrown into deeper confusion when she learns her recently divorced parents both plan to remarry.	a,n	10-15	Yes
180. SM	2 stepbrothers	Divorce	Nina is caught in the middle. Her new math teacher is her father's wife. Her mother dislikes her father. She's afraid her father left her mother because of the SM. Her friends plot revenge on the stepmother/teacher.	a,d,f,j, m,o	11-14	No
181. SM	5 ½ sibs	Divorce	13 yr. old Natalie's life undergoes chaotic changes when her stepmother has quintuplets. Her father neglects her needs & those of her new stepmother. Natalie returns to her mothers to live.	a,e,j,m, o,t	10-14	Yes
182. SM	0	Divorce	Marly hates her mother & runs away to her father & stepmother. Develops crush on teacher, gets into trouble at school.	m,r	11-15	No
183. SF/ SM	1 stepbrother	Divorce	Leigh has been acting since she was a baby. When Leigh's mother remarries, she acquires a stepbrother, Peter, who is a hemophiliac, & moves from New York City to Long Island to lead the life of a normal teenager. All she knows, however, is fantasy & so Peter becomes her coach. Leigh is mature & has excellent relations with both her parents & her stepfather, but she keeps finding herself out of sync with the events of a small town high school.	a,d,h	12-15	Yes
184. SF	0	Divorce	Simple book relating how a young boy adjusted to his stepfather & the changes in his life caused by his mother's	a,g,h,j, n,o,p,t	7-10	Yes

Stepmother Stepfather	Stepsiblings # Sex	Stepfamily Formed Due to Death or Divorce	Summary	[d]Themes	Suggested Age Range of Readers	Recommended
			remarriage. Deals with issues raised by clinicians (e.g., what to call a stepparent, sharing with stepsibling, having enough love for everyone, multiple Christmas).			
185. SM	0	Death	Tormented by his mother's death, his father's rejection, & his grandparent's inability to understand him, Mark finally finds new strengths & purpose in his acquaintance with a young quadriplegic (Connie) with whom he shares an interest in nature. Set in Australia, the story is woven around the symbol of the albatross.	d,g,u	14 up	Yes
186. SF	none	Divorce/Death	Emotionally disturbed Cloris remains true to her dead father's memory & plots against her mother remarrying.	a,d,g,o,t	11 up	Yes, highly
187. SF	none	Divorce/Death	Emotionally disturbed stepchild is resentful of stepfather. She succeeds in breaking up the remarriage. Sequel to *Cloris & the Creeps*.	a,d,g,n	12 up	No
188. Doesn't apply	0	Death/Divorce	Cloris, clinging to memory of father's death, attempts to control mother's social life. Sequel to *Cloris and the Creeps* and *Cloris and the Freaks*.	a,d,g	12 up	Yes
189. SF (cohabit)	0	Divorce	Eddie has a fierce temper, the "ape," he attempts to control. His mother's live-in boyfriend is presented very negatively and Eddie fights with him causing him to walk out. Blue collar setting filled with mentally unhealthy characters. Negative view of stepfamily.	d,s	13-18	No
190. SF	0	Death	Samantha, a middle child who envies certain qualities in her older brother & younger sister, discovers her mother is planning to remarry and schemes to prevent it.	n,o	8-12	Yes

Stepmother Stepfather	Stepsiblings # Sex	Stepfamily Formed Due to Death or Divorce	Summary	[d]Themes	Suggested Age Range of Readers	Recommended
191. SM	0	Death	Billie leaves her Arkansas home because she can't get along with her stepmother. On the bus ride to Chicago, where she is going to live with an older sister who is married, Billie meets a man who gives her a gift of a box of rocks. The excitement begins when it is discovered that one of the rocks is a stolen diamond & the crook arrives in Chicago to find it (and Billie). Billie learns that there are other difficult people besides her stepmother & there are nice stepmothers, too (her new girlfriend has one).	n	12 up	Yes
192. SM	0	Death	Carrie is upset at the thought of her father remarrying & acts obnoxiously. It's apparent that she's a nice child at heart when she becomes attached to Grace, an elderly neighbor. Sharon (stepmother) wins Carrie over by understanding Carrie's concern for Grace when Grace has a heart attack.	g,n,o,r	10-16	Yes
193. SM/ SF	1 stepsister	Death/divorce	Silly book about several girls who belong to the Zodiac Club and think their zodiac sign is very important. One of the members, Elizabeth, whose mother died, becomes a stepchild & stepsib when her father marries. Eliza. thinks Liz (her stepsister) is after her boyfriend but the 2 girls come to an understanding and Liz goes off to boarding school. Situations are contrived & obvious.	h,n,o,p	12-15	No
194. SF	0	Death	Art Byfield runs away from an angry confrontation with his stepfather & ends up in California working on a ranch for crusty old Yuma Schoonover. Yuma, a former convict, raises horses for movies and television. Art's 6 month stay with Yuma is one in which he learns many important lessons.	b,e,g,n, o,r	12-16	Yes

Stepmother Stepfather	Stepsiblings # Sex	Stepfamily Formed Due to Death or Divorce	Summary	dThemes	Suggested Age Range of Readers	Recommended
195. SM	1 stepsister	Death	MCs life as a Jew after Nazi occupation of Holland is made even more difficult by the loss of her beloved older sister & her father's remarriage.	g,j,l,m, n,s	12-16	No
196. SF	0	Divorce	Girl attends boarding school & adjusts to the nonstructured learning environment & others at the school.	n	11 up	Yes
197. SF	1 stepbrother 1 stepsister	Divorce	Child abuse by biological mother is the focus; stepbrother intervenes as does stepfather & stepgrandmother.	h,m,p,r	10 up	Yes
198. SF	2 stepsisters	Death	Billy is unhappy because his mother is going to remarry; he & a friend build a hideout up the mountain so Billy can run away & live there. A brief, fast moving story with little relevance to most children because of it's mountain setting & the fact that Billy's parents were quite calm about his being missing for 2 days. Little insight into the characters or stepfamily dynamics.	n	9-12	No
199. SM	1 stepsister	Death	MC unhappy about father's remarriage; develops relationship with recluse & learns some painful lessons in life. Set in England.	h,n,p	10-15	Yes
200. SF	0	Divorce	A teenage boy who works winters as a caretaker for houses in a Long Island resort area suddenly finds himself also taking care of his alcoholic father & a wealthy runaway girl. Stepfamily is very incidental to this story about a boy coping with his father's alcoholism & his fear of going crazy. The book might be helpful for children of alcoholics.	k	14 up	No
201. SF	1 half-brother	Abandonment	Should Greg Yardley, the main character, go to live with his biological father (who is wealthy & can offer many opportunities) or stay with his family in a small town? After going	a,m,n,v	12 up	Yes

Stepmother Stepfather	Stepsiblings # Sex	Stepfamily Formed Due to Death or Divorce	Summary	[d]Themes	Suggested Age Range of Readers	Recommended
			through an emotionally exhausting orderal he comes to the decision that family is not biological, but nurturant. Story is of adoption rather than step.			
202. SF	0	Divorce	Leah lives with her stepfather, Moe, who at 70 odd years is older than her grandmother. (Leah's mother died shortly after marrying Moe and both he and her grandmother wanted Leah.) Matt, his parents & twin sisters move in next door & Leah discovers Matt is an unwed father when he goes to California & returns with his baby daughter. Leah becomes obsessed with the baby & things go downhill from there. Little motivation for any of the characters.	d,u	16 up	No
203. SF/ SM	1 sister	Divorce	15 yr. old Katie tries to cope with many changes in her life when her actress mother acquires a serious suitor, her best friend drifts away into other interests, her dance teacher encourages her hopes of a dance career, & the boy she's always admired suddenly notices her.	t	13 up	Yes
204. SF	0	Divorce	Becky, her mom, & her new cat, Shyster, leave the city to spend a few weeks living in the country with Arthur, her mom's boyfriend. Becky doesn't want to live with Arthur because her dad might not be able to find her "when" he comes back. On the farm Becky comes to grips with her feelings about Arthur & about her disappeared father. Touches on some important concerns of children as they move into a step household. Arthur is a grade school teacher, kind, understanding, & yet Becky doesn't really like him.	a,d,f,n	9-12	Yes

Stepmother Stepfather	Stepsiblings # Sex	Stepfamily Formed Due to Death or Divorce	Summary	[d]Themes	Suggested Age Range of Readers	Recommended
205. SM/ SF	3 ½ sibs	Divorce	17 yr. old Cass misunderstands her divorced parents until she discovers the secret they've been keeping from her: She has a severely handicapped terminally ill younger sister. Cass displays typical adolescent stepchild irrationality. Objectionable scene where Gideon Jones (who later becomes a boyfriend) rapes Cass thinking that's what she wants.	a,c,e,g, h,j,l,m, o,r,u	13-18	Yes, with reservation
206. SM	0	Divorce	Main character, David, lives with mother & is extremely sympathetic to her problems. When he realizes his father is interested in another woman he becomes angry because he feels it is unjust for his father to happily marry while he sees his mother as being an overworked, overburdened victim. David sets out to sabotage his father's relationship with the father's girlfriend.	a,d,e,f,g, h,l,m,n, o,p	13-18	No
207. SF	0	Biological father unknown	Shelley, a PINS (person in need of supervision) is a runaway who is bounced from foster homes to detention centers & training schools. Her home life is terrible and her stepfather is the stereotyped lecher.	i,k,s	12 up	No
208. SF	1 stepsister	Divorce	Robyn Adam's name was changed to her stepfather's name when her mother remarried because her father was in prison (he had killed his stepfather when drunk). As the book opens, Robert Adam is getting out of prison & Robyn has arranged to help him adjust on the outside. Her mother is so upset over this she tells Robyn if she continues to see her father she must move out. Robyn moves in with her father and sees that his problems are beyond her ability to help. Good char-	a,d,e,h, l,m,p,t	14 up	Yes

Stepmother Stepfather	Stepsiblings # Sex	Stepfamily Formed Due to Death or Divorce	Summary	[d]Themes	Suggested Age Range of Readers	Recommended
			acter development, realistic stepfamily dynamics. Shelley Clark of *Run Shelley Run* is a minor character in the book.			
209. SM	1 half-brother	Death	Barbara whose mother died when she was quite young is resentful at first of her father's remarriage. She adjusts rapidly however in this outdated book that seems almost comical compared to more recent books for adolescents. The story of pampered bored teenagers growing up goes nowhere. Big families are idealized, nice girls seldom kiss boys, the most popular boys in school are **always** the captain of the football & basketball team, etc.	b,e	12-16	No
210. SM	0	Death	Shawn has a stepmother, but she plays no role in the book. Shawn doesn't want to live with his father and wife in Arizona after his mother dies. Instead, he wants to live with his grandfather who is learning to speak after larynx surgery. Interestingly, his father is never consulted about this. Shawn spends the summer trying to recover from his mother's death & his own botched suicide attempt.	g,n	14 up	No
211. SF	1 stepsib	Divorce	16 yr. old Tammy is caught between her materialistic mother & stepfather & her saintlike father who is a teacher. Her father dies at the end of the book, and the reader is left with no clue to Tammy's future. Characters are all drawn very black or white.	m,n	11-16	Yes
212. SF (common law)	0	Death	A depressing story with an unrealistic ending of a 6th grade girl who establishes an increasingly close relationship with a couple on a nearby ranch & comes to realize there is nothing left between her-	i,k,m,s	10-12	No

Stepmother Stepfather	Stepsiblings # Sex	Stepfamily Formed Due to Death or Divorce	Summary	[d]Themes	Suggested Age Range of Readers	Recommended
			self & her alcoholic mother. Clyde, who lives with Benicia's mother, is an unpleasant lecherous person who intimidates Benicia, robs banks with the help of Benicia's mother, & leaves the country thus abandoning Benicia to shift for herself.			
213. SM	2 stepsibs	Death	A psychodrama of a boy who thinks his stepmother is a bear who is trying to drain his creativity. His stepmother paints & Jason writes poems. She also had emotional difficulties as a child & understands him well. He comes to realize he is more like her than he is like his father or biomother who didn't understand him.	a,d,g,n, r,t	11-16	Yes
214. SM/ SF	1 stepbrother	Death/divorce	Razz falls hard for T.J. and struggles when her mother & his father marry. Jealousy & the changed relationship create problems for her. Deals fairly tastefully with stepsibs attraction to each other.	h,i,m,n, p,t	13-17	Yes
215. Doesn't apply	0	Separation	Jody's 15th summer brings major changes in her father's love life & her own, when she becomes attracted to his lady friend's son. Jody's mother is off "finding herself."	no themes	12-15	Yes
216. SM	1 half-brother	Death	April resents her father & the fact she must live with him after her mother dies. He despises her new boyfriend.	a,g,e,l,u	13-17	No
217. SM	0	Death	Girl with weight problem resents intrusion of new stepmother. Only makes friends with her after the father is killed and the SM crippled from a wreck.	n,o,r	11-15	Yes
218. SF/ SM	1 stepbrother	Not stated	An uneasy friendship with the strange, constantly angry new girl in her neighborhood leads 11 yr. old Janie Potter to discover a hidden cache of money and stolen property.	g,h,n,t	8-12	Yes

Stepmother Stepfather	Stepsiblings # Sex	Stepfamily Formed Due to Death or Divorce	Summary	[d]Themes	Suggested Age Range of Readers	Recommended
219. SF	1 half-sister	Divorce	Carolyn tries to deal with the knowledge her half-brother is a thief. Richard's biological father has only sent him a few cards over the years &, though promising to come see him, never does. Richard knows he looks like his father and comes to feel he's also "no good" like his father. Since he can't possibly be as "perfect" as his stepfather he ends up stealing through the influence of Flimflam, a friend. The book might help some stepchildren and parents realize the sort of twisted thinking that may go on in children's heads when they know very little about their biological parents.	b,d	12-16	Yes
220. SF	2 stepsisters	Death	Right after the wedding Libby and her new stepfamily take a trip to Europe; the book is about the trip. At the end of the book Libby's mother breaks her foot and all problems become magically resolved. The story has little substance & the ending is very unrealistic.	h	10-13	0
221. SF	0	Never married	Set in New Zealand. The story begins with Harper & her mother leaving the man they've been living with because he has tried to molest Harper several times. The rest of the book is filled with their adventures or misadventures, and Harper's finally learning who her father is (a man much younger than her mother who is a homosexual and whom they had lived happily with when Harper was younger). She gains a stepfather—a man she really picked. Book contains some nice imagery but would probably not appeal to American young people—they would not identify with it.	d,e,g,i, n,o	14 up	No

Stepmother Stepfather	Stepsiblings # Sex	Stepfamily Formed Due to Death or Divorce	Summary	dThemes	Suggested Age Range of Readers	Recommended
222. SM	1 stepsister 1 half brother	Never married	A 15 yr. old who lives with her mother, an ardent feminist, in a women's commune, begins to discover how others live when she visits her father, a successful architect, for the first time.	a,d,j, m,n	12 up	Yes
223. SF	1 half brother	Death	Supernatural tale of Sam who had always been jealous of his half brother, Humphrey, a famous child prodigy piano player. At 15, Humphrey looks older than he is & can no longer draw crowds. His parents come up with a plan to have Sam write music, drug Humphrey, & make Hump believe he wrote the music in a trance. The son of the dead composer whose music Sam was copying shows up & they find out the dead composer has been working through Sam's head & Humphrey's hands. They escape from their obnoxious stage parents & go live on a secret island with Lazlo, the composer's son.	h,m,o	13-18	Yes, as an adventure story
224. SM	1 stepsister	Divorce	A 15 yr. old tennis player's (Buddy) experiences in the world of competitive sports help him come to terms with his parents' divorce, his first romance, & his own ambition. The book has more to do with "stage (tennis) mothers" and competition than stepfamilies.	a	12-14	Yes
225. SF	0	Never married	Lacey moves from Colo. to the Appalachians of North Carolina with her mother & David (who serves as her SF). Campbell (the mother) left there 10 yrs. before because her mother was trying to get legal custody of Lacey. David goes about trying to "melt" hard feelings between Campbell and Grandmom but is killed in a car accident before it's accomplished.	g,n,u,r	10-16	Yes, highly

Stepmother Stepfather	Stepsiblings # Sex	Stepfamily Formed Due to Death or Divorce	Summary	[d]Themes	Suggested Age Range of Readers	Recommended
			Excellent story of family values, stubborness, and resolving of family differences. Stepfamily dynamics are all positive, extended family dynamics are not. Lacey meets her biofather & has no feelings toward him. David is who she feels is her father.			
226. SM	0	Death	13 yr. old Margaret finds a mysterious, shadowy figure watching her as she searches for a lost gold nugget from an abandoned mine.	u,t	10-16	Yes
227. SF	0	Divorce	Lloyd, a sixth grader, was the strikeout king and always chosen last for recess softball games. Lloyd had no friends, was a discipline problem at school & was overweight and immature. Lloyd has a "secret," however. He is actually a superb batter. His stubborn refusal to participate in the game, using his real hitting skills is finally broken by the prodding of Kirby, a new friend who accidentally uncovered Lloyd's secret, & by his friendship with Ancil, a new girl in school. Stepfamily issues are peripheral to this story, although there are frequent references to stepfathers; Lloyd has had two in the past & Ancil has one. Excellent portrayal of an enmeshed single-parent family.	h,m	10-13	Yes
228. SF	0	Death	Sequel to *Last Was Lloyd*, chronicling the adventures of Lloyd & Ancil during the summer following sixth grade. The focus of this story is Ancil who in convinced that her biological father, an MIA, is still alive in Vietnam. The problems of a child who must undergo several transitions (moving, new school, new stepfather) are honestly por-	a,d,f,g, n,t,u	11-16	Yes, highly

Stepmother Stepfather	Stepsiblings # Sex	Stepfamily Formed Due to Death or Divorce	Summary	[d]Themes	Suggested Age Range of Readers	Recommended
			trayed. The thought-processes & emotional growth of pre-adolescents are presented with great skill.			
229. SM	0	Divorce	A shy 15 yr. old girl, more at ease on the sports field than anywhere else, tries to cope with new feelings and a gradual understanding of herself, her divorced parents, & other people around her.	f,n	11 up	Yes
230. SM/ SF	1 stepsister	Death 1 family, divorce other	Stepsister tries to get "even" with new family through witch-craft. Entertaining but not very realistic.	a,b,h,j,p	10-14	Yes
231. SF	1 stepbrother	Divorce	Stepbrothers being split by second divorce; stuttering problem of main character is featured. Strong stepsibling dynamics.	n,q	12 up	Yes
232. SF/ SM	1 stepbrother 1 stepsister	Divorce	Twelve-year-old Andrea, whose parents have divorced & re-married, discusses the complexities of her new, larger family. This book is a "photo essay." It contains many issues in relatively few pages.	a,b,d,f, g,h,j,m, n,o,s,t,u	12 up	Yes
233. SF	0	Death	Lotte resolves not to go to America with her mother & new stepfather because of her loyalty to Denmark & her father's memory. Because her mother overcame her fear of flying to be at Lotte's bedside when she became ill in Denmark, Lotte decides to go to America after all.	g,n,u	10-14	No
234. SM	0	Death	Story of the 4 Cares children; principally the adventure of the three older children. At the end of the book the children gain a stepmother much to the delight of Jane & Edie & the disgruntlement of Theodore who announces that her arrival will mean the end of many pleasures, the laying down of many laws, and "a lot of new squawky babies." Un-	r	10-13	No

Stepmother Stepfather	Stepsiblings # Sex	Stepfamily Formed Due to Death or Divorce	Summary	[d]Themes	Suggested Age Range of Readers	Recommended
			believably, even Theodore is won over by the gentle woman who accepts them all and "stands up to Father." Slow moving book.			
235. SM	1 half-sister	Death	The author uses eight separate incidents to show one year's adventures of a wealthy family in the early 1900's in America. By looking into the minds of the different children at different times in that year he shows the reader the thought processes of each of the characters.	o,r	10-12	Yes
236. SM	2 half-sisters	Death	Third in a series of books about the Cares family who lived in a small Massachusetts town in the 1900s. The principle character is Edie, the youngest of the original Cares family. The story also includes Father, Madam (the stepmother), the new half-sisters, Edie's 3 siblings & their various nurses & all the household help. Stepfamily dynamics are barely mentioned & there is a distinct lack of theme in the book. Slow moving book.	no themes	10-13	No
237. SM	1 stepsibling	Death	The MC is a girl who becomes friends with a boy who lives with his stepmother. She presumably sleeps with almost every man & neglects her stepson & daughter. The husband/father is away at war.	a,d,h,i,k, m,s	13-16	No
238. SF	1 stepbrother	Death	Rachel's attempts to promote family togetherness in her new stepfamily leads to quarrels.	b,d,i,p,u	12-15	No
239. SF/ SM	1 stepsister	Death/divorce	PJ's father was killed in a fire & she doesn't want her mother to marry another fireman, especially the father of her boyfriend's exgirlfriend. A silly contrived & predictable romance story.	h,o,p	12-15	Yes, with reservations

Stepmother Stepfather	Stepsiblings # Sex	Stepfamily Formed Due to Death or Divorce	Summary	[d]Themes	Suggested Age Range of Readers	Recommended
240. SM	1 half brother	Death	After the death of her beloved grandfather, 16 yr. old Caroline resists change, spending her time with an elderly grandmother or alone, until a flamboyant new girl at school draws her reluctantly into a friendship. It's the new girl who lives in a stepfamily.	d,g,n	11-17	Yes
241. SF	0	(mother not previously married)	Magnus (MC) is 9; he was born when his mother was 16. His father was married to someone else but sends money to help support Magnus. Leffe, an alcoholic, ex-con, moves in with them and they form a family. Leffe, however, begins drinking again, disappears and then returns & finally ends up in jail again. A sad, depressing book written from the 9 yr. olds point of view but not a book for children. Alcoholism, poverty & immaturity are central to the theme.	k,o	14 up	Yes, with reservations
242. SF	0	Death	After her father dies, Seely & her family move to the city where her mother feels life will be easier, but life in the city presents a new set of problems that the family has not encountered before.	n	12 up	Yes
243. SF	0	Death	10 yr. old Josh, who finds his private school unbearable, joins forces with an elderly man in tending injured birds. Positive view of stepfamilies.	r	11-13	Yes
244.	1 stepbrother	Death	Typical of the novels written in the first ⅓ of the 20th century involving young girl detectives (young girl being defined as anyone unmarried or childless & under the age of 30) who are whizzes at solving a mystery and setting everything straight in 250 pages. Designed for the older upper	s	12-17	No

Stepmother Stepfather	Stepsiblings # Sex	Stepfamily Formed Due to Death or Divorce	Summary	[d]Themes	Suggested Age Range of Readers	Recommended
			to middle class adolescent of the 20's, this book is filled with negative references to Blacks and steprelations.			
245. SM	1 stepsister 1 stepbrother	Death	Adolescent girl, trying to develop identity especially in her relationship with her stepmother and stepsister, who have a different background and values.	e,h,n,o, p,t	13 up	Yes
246. SF	0	Death	While visiting his mother and new stepfather whom he hates (for no apparent reason) an English teenager is terrorized by 3 scarecrows embodying people who met violent death and who silently threaten the whole family. Simon communicates with his dead father & engages in emotionally disturbed behavior attempting to break up the remarriage. The English terminology and slang would be difficult for some readers.	b,d,g,o	14 up	No
247. SM	1 ½ sib	Death/divorce	After the murder by drug-overdose of a fellow student, Beverly breaks away from the fast crowd she joined after her mother's suicide & moving in with her father and stepmother. She finds herself friendless and full of guilt until she meets Derek who helps her come to terms with the past & look with some hope to the future.	a,b,g,k, l,m,n,p, t,d	14 up	Yes, Highly
248. SM	0	Death	Father remarries 3 years after death of children's mother to a woman who is the "perfect" stepmother. The story takes place at the beginning of the depression (though the family is very wealthy) and the book is dated. A great deal is made of the children referring to the stepmother as "Mother." Pointless, unrealistic story.	no themes	8-11	No

Stepmother Stepfather	Stepsiblings # Sex	Stepfamily Formed Due to Death or Divorce	Summary	[d]Themes	Suggested Age Range of Readers	Recommended
249. SF	1 stepbrother 1 stepsister	Death	Story of a New York City teenager struggling with changes due to her mother's remarriage (i.e., moving to a small midwestern town for her senior year of high school, acquiring a stepfather, stepbrother & stepsister, having to share a room, etc.) Realistic stepfamily dynamics; even the pets have trouble adjusting to each other at first.	a,b,g,h, n,o,p,t	12 up	Yes
250. SM/ SF	6 total children	Death	Adjusting to complex blended stepfamily. Scotland is the setting. Unrealistic solution to problems.	b,h,p,n	12 up	Yes
251. SF/ SM	6 children	Not stated	Merging of two families & cultures (American and English). Parents leave on trip because children are fighting and leave children to settle things on their own. A storm unites them.	e,h,p,n	10-14	Yes
252. SF/ SM	2 stepbrothers		8 yr. old Mitzi finds out just how great her stepbrother Frederick really is when they accompany her mother to New Mexico to work on an archaeological dig for the summer. Nice story with stepsibs being kind to each other & looking out for each other's welfare.	h,o,t	8-12	Yes
253. SF/ SM	2 stepbrothers	Divorce	Mitzi must get used to her newly acquired family due to her mother's remarriage. She has an 11 yr. old stepbrother, 3 yr. old stepbrother and step-grandmother who all move into Mitzi's house. This adjustment takes place while her mother and new husband are on their 2 week honeymoon.	b,h,n,o, p,u	8-11	Yes
254. SF/ SM	2 stepbrothers	Divorce	Mitzi becomes friends with the elephant keeper at the zoo, from whom she hopes to learn how to train big animals so she can get a Saint Bernard puppy.	t,u	8-12	Yes

Stepmother Stepfather	Stepsiblings # Sex	Stepfamily Formed Due to Death or Divorce	Summary	[d]Themes	Suggested Age Range of Readers	Recommended
255. SF/ SM	2 stepbrothers	Death/divorce	The disruption of the mother-daughter relationship & family harmony from the perspective of an 8 yr. old girl. Includes the problems of loss of status & sibling rivalry.	b,h,n,o, p,r,u	8-10	Yes
256. SM	0	Death	Silly story of 3 brothers actively searching for a mother. Slapstick; too unrealistic and not funny or original enough to be good fantasy.	e,l	6-10	Yes, with reservations
257. SM	half-sibling expected	Divorce	Child tries to figure out why her parents' divorced, how they fell "out of love." Her stepmother's pregnancy ends her fantasy to reunite her parents & helps her look at the future more realistically. Humor is used well to present a sound plot.	a,f,j,m, n,t	12 up	Yes, highly
258. SF	0	Death	While Bernie's mother prepares for the second wedding, and his sister Celia rehearses for her starring role in the school play, he concentrates on getting the $99 he needs to carry out his plan to go live with his grandfather in Florida. He must also learn to cope with daily hassles such as asthma, algebra, his mom's disgustingly cheerful boyfriend, a new girlfriend, & his stressed-out sister.	a,d,g,n	12-15	Yes
259. SF	1 stepbrother	Divorce	Mother of stepbrother is unreasonable, stepsister's plot to allow him to live with them. Stepfather cares genuinely for the welfare of the girls as well as his son. Unrealistic story.	a,h,j,m, p,q	10-14	Yes
260. S/grand-mother	0	Death	The summer before Emily's sixth grade year is suddenly ruined when her widowed grandfather returns from a trip to L.A. with a new wife. Emily, who has been grandpa's "best girl," is jealous.	g,n,o,u	10-16	Yes

Stepmother Stepfather	Stepsiblings # Sex	Stepfamily Formed Due to Death or Divorce	Summary	[d]Themes	Suggested Age Range of Readers	Recommended
261. SF	1 stepbrother	Death	During a summer in an abandoned mining town, Katie's relationship with a rebellious stepbrother improves as they probe the past to find out why there seem to be ghosts, literally, beneath their feet.	b,g,h,n, p,t	10-15	Yes
262. SF	0	Death	Torn between devotion for & jealousy of her beautiful & much-admired invalid sister, 12 yr. old Caroline's drab self-image begins to change when she meets the glamorous Lillian MacGregor who makes her feel important.	l,o	12-15	Yes
263. SM	0	Death	Gloomy Freudian book about sibling rivalry that ends with no hope of resolution. Sara (13) wants to get rid of Jenny (9) everyone's favorite & hatches a plan, making it appear that Jenny is writing messages to herself from her dead mother.	g,o	10 up	No
264. SM	1 half sister	Divorce/death	A sad but moving story of Beth, whose mother killed herself a number of years after Beth's parent's divorced. Beth then moved in with her father, stepmother and baby half-sister. The story is of adjustments — Linda, the stepmother, to no longer working & having a self identity & becoming a mother to 2 daughters, not just the 1 she had planned on; Beth — to a new school, a romance, the stepfamily & finally to some resolution of her mother's death and mourning. A good book with no heroes; real people with realistic emotions and conflicts.	a,g,d,g,l m,n,o, p,t	13 up	Yes
265. SF	0	Death	Stepfamily is incidental to this dated story which is mainly about poor judgement & immaturity in teenagers. Liz is unhappy at home, dates Sean, wealthy and also unhappy, and becomes pregnant. Sean offers	b,c,s	15 up	No

Stepmother Stepfather	Stepsiblings # Sex	Stepfamily Formed Due to Death or Divorce	Summary	[d]Themes	Suggested Age Range of Readers	Recommended
			to marry Liz but backs out after talking with his father. Liz gets an abortion and because she bleeds heavily afterwards her family finds out. She cuts herself off from her friends.			

NOTE: [a]MC = age of Main Character

  [b]MC = sex of Main Character (F = Female, M = Male)

  [c]Quality ratings: 1 = No merit

  2 = Some merit

  3 = Average merit

  4 = Above average merit

  5 = Superior merit

  [d]Themes: a = divided loyalty

  b = discipline issues

  c = pseudomutuality

  d = unresolved feelings for absent parent

  e = unrealistic expectations

  f = desire for parents to reunite

  g = loss and mourning

  h = stepsiblings relationship

  i = sexual issues

  j = membership in two households

  k = alcoholism

  l = guilt

  m = relationship with biological parent/s

  n = child's adjustment to change

  o = jealousy

  p = merging of families

  q = custody issues

  r = stepparent as rescuer

  s = negative image of stepfamily

  t = realistic stepfamily dynamics

  u = extended family

INDEX

131